Today is
Yesterday's Tomorrow

Best Wishes

Mary MacDonald

Today is
Yesterday's Tomorrow

Mary MacDonald

The Pentland Press Limited
Edinburgh • Cambridge • Durham

First published in 1994 by
The Pentland Press Ltd.
1 Hutton Close
South Church
Bishop Auckland
Durham

ISBN 1 85821 194 8

Typeset by CBS, Felixstowe, Suffolk
Printed and bound by Antony Rowe Ltd., Chippenham

Dedicated to my grandson,
Colin Hughes, and his sister, Lynn Hughes,
who both encouraged me at all times and
provided me with invaluable assistance.

Foreword

Today is Yesterday's Tomorrow is an honest, genuine and sometimes moving account of incidents in Mary MacDonald's life. Written with the express purpose of leaving something for her children and grandchildren, it is nevertheless a book which will be enjoyed by other readers.

From the days when she was a schoolgirl in a croft in Wester Ross in 'a sturdy cottage sitting at the bottom of a grassy knoll' to her adventures in foreign countries, she describes a great many incidents, some amusing, some sad, but all very interesting. Although tragedies occur she is never sorry for herself; in fact there is an over-riding sense of fun throughout.

Her children and grandchildren, while enjoying the many surprises and good laughs in the book, will at the same time be very proud of the author.

A. D. Cunningham

Chapter 1

Why is it, that having visited most of Europe and enjoyed the sunshine of the Canary Islands, my mind in times of reflection, always goes back to that croft in the hills on the west coast of Scotland, where the labour of love was plentiful?

Looking back, they must have been really hard, hard times for my parents. But no matter how I probe into my memory, I cannot recall even one moment of grumble. Wish that I could, as it would make that life more real for me. Did they have the skill to hide those grumbles?

I do not recall the exchange of money, it must have been all barter. I do know that eggs, home-made butter and cheese, were exchanged for sugar, tea and cereals about ever two weeks; I helped to carry some of those baskets to the nearest grocery store, four miles away! And glad I was to do so, to be rewarded with strips of liquorice. Although this was a luxury, I got fed up with it, but it was my own fault, as the first time I was asked would I like a sweet, I said: 'Yes please!', and pointed to the strips of liquorice among the array of sweets. Simply out of curiosity, I suppose, as I had never seen them before and I wondered what they were. Why, black sweets, of course.

My mother and I were then taken into the parlour behind the shop and given a cup of tea with cake and assorted biscuits, scrumptious! Before we set off on our return journey of four miles, why did I not slip a biscuit or two into my pocket? Because the Commandments were implanted in my childhood, and it is difficult to shake them off as the years go by.

I see the white-washed croft house, very pretty, sparsely furnished and smelling of fresh paint. Who was the painter? Why, mother of

1

course, jack of all trades; from spinning, to knitting and baking; and they were only the inside chores! One couldn't count on one's hand the outside ones.

The smoke from the sturdy cottage sitting at the bottom of the grassy knoll, spiralled into the blue sky; always a welcome sign to any visitor. And the clothes flapping in the breeze, all hand washed, with the aid of a washing board. Life Buoy soap, and a blue bag. I still do not know what that blue bag contained to make the whites whiter than white.

Crofting is a way of life, not a business. It is complex and chancy and certainly no occupation for fools. The main cash flow is through the sale of stock, so it is wiser to have quality instead of quantity. A garden is a moral extravagance, animals have more importance – except pet lambs, who are greedy and demanding and grow into pet sheep, and think humans are only there for the purposes of feeding them. And no matter how happily they are grazing, the minute a door is opened, they rush in, in search of titbits. They always shove and butt you, so you learn to carry something in your apron pocket to make a quick get-away!

A crofter cannot always attend market or accompany his beasts. He sometimes has to share transport and sell at a lower price rather than bring an animal back unsold from a distant market, facing heavy freight charges.

Do I regret having been brought up on a croft? Certainly not. I did not relish all the hard work at the time, but I benefited from it in later years, when life was harder still. I had the best of two worlds, having lived in a croft in the hills, and also a croft by the sea.

What were the treasure troves in those days? Why, old doors, sheets of corrugated iron, any piece of discarded wood. What for? Well, there was the hen-house to be extended, or the barn reinforced, or a wind-break for lambs. A crofter had to be a mason, a joiner, a farmer and a miner, the latter meaning he had to produce fuel for the fire. But thankfully, in our area, there was plenty of peat and moss not too far away.

Village children always loved to come and visit me. There was always a thicket of wood that only we children could get through and no adult could penetrate. But inside there was a mossy patch where we could hide and play houses all day long, or any other game we chose, and nobody would be aware that we were even there. Did our parents worry as to where we were? Evidently not. There were only ourselves or tinkers who might occupy those secluded spots; harmless people who had lovely dogs, and children with beautiful unkempt curly hair. How I used to envy them, as I had straight hair. Out of curiosity, we would venture towards their tents or wigwams, to try and find out what was inside the three-legged pots, swinging on a tripod and giving off a succulent smell. I was lucky enough one day to be offered a helping of rabbit stew which I refused, saying I was not hungry, only to be handed a scone and black treacle, which I could not refuse, but I made the excuse I had to go home. Possibly some bird, or animal, further along the road, appreciated what I had discarded.

Mole hills fascinated me, and I used to sit hoping to catch a glimpse of who, or what kind of animal made such lovely little mounds, but capture them I never did.

To open a peat hag, or moss, you begin by stripping, or skimming, the top layer of turf along the edge of the bank until you come to the peaty earth. Peats are then dug out in layers, depending on how far down you can go, before too much water collects. The wet peats are laid out on the bank to dry out then they are set up in little pyramids so that the wind can blow through. When they are thoroughly dry they can be as hard as coal. They are then stacked beside the house and, if well built, can keep out the rain.

Though very hard work, it can also be a pleasure, depending on the weather. A picnic is a must, when working all day in a team. There is no time to moan and it is such hard, physical work you are so hungry that no matter what the picnic consists of you will eat it.

You become more tired, but it is a case of just another row or two to spread. Exhaustion creeps in but the scent of the bog-myrtle around soon revives you. Straightening your back you then gaze in wonder at a certain butterfly, which you have never seen before, and you follow its flight for a minute or two, until the boss or father says: 'Come on, come on, you can't spread peat standing up', and then you sink your feet further down into the peat moss, giving them a wonderful tan, throw up a few more at bank level, and think of that glorious peat fire on a winter's evening, and forget the pain in your back. After all, the nearest coal depot was ten miles away, and we had no transport apart from the old mare.

Every highland home had a framed sampler of 'The Lord Is My Shepherd' on the wall. I was always curious as to why so many had them, even young couples. The answer I got, from whom I will not say, was that it was normal practice for this to be given as a wedding gift.

We had very little of material luxury goods. Yet, should I not count our menu of those days as luxury food? It consisted of fresh, unsalted butter, cottage cheese or crowdie, and plenty of fresh milk. Do you wonder the medicine box only held castor oil, a few bandages and a bar of carbolic soap? Oh, how I wish I could turn back the clock and show appreciation for the love and attention we got, and took for granted.

We grudgingly went to feed the pet lamb, equally grudgingly we went to look for eggs laid outside in secret nests. Why? Because we were too busy erecting swings, climbing trees, fishing, gathering wild flowers, bathing and swimming.

All croft houses must bulge with homeliness: the dogs love the cats, the cats love the hens and everybody loves the chickens. What of that very inquisitive hen, who pokes her nose into everything, even into the kitchen on baking day, hoping to catch the odd grain of oatmeal that falls from the table, before the bannock reaches the girdle? Nobody could ever think of putting her in the pot at the end of her days! She must be given a decent burial, despite the fact that she was such a nuisance. How many visitors have tripped over her when they have called for a cup of tea? She always seemed to be hovering around the lobby as if listening to some gossip.

The iron kettle never seemed to be off the boil. Always singing by the side of that much polished grate. What a welcome sign for the uninvited guest who had walked several miles, as the lid went: 'plop, plop', as if to say: 'Come in, come in'. The whole scene always oozed with hospitality, even with the annoying hen, and the wagging of the dogs' tails. How refreshing to look back on those scenes.

Were there only twelve months in the year then, in those far away days, and how did everyone accomplish so much by hand, without machinery? There was the sowing season, with a canvas apron draped around one's neck, and with a certain swing of each arm scattering the seed. The lambing season, the chicken hatching, the blanket tramping days, (that was fun), the hay making, sheep shearing, the harvest gathering, the potato lifting, and storing, all by hand! No wonder our hands and feet were like leather as we seldom wore footwear in summer.

No sleeping pills in those days, in the croft way of life. I'm beginning to think the more advanced the culture, the less advanced the people.

We now moved to what some would call a more civilized area by the sea. It certainly had its advantages, in as much as we had an important addition to our income, if we so wished. Gathering whelks for Billingsgate Market, they were collected in sacks and sent by train to a chosen merchant. This was also back-breaking work, and at the mercy of the tides. To keep them fresh, they had to be left in the sacks in the water until the gathering was complete and ready for transport. This was a risky business and an afternoon's work could disappear overnight.

The acquiring of an iron sink and piped cold water did not bring the joy I thought it might as there seemed to be more satisfaction in carrying two pails of water from the well. That done, you felt you had achieved something more than the simple turn of your wrist to produce cold water.

Was I suffering from homesickness for that croft in the hills? I sat and thought of the hills, which reared up on each side, with the sinking sun splashing on the bracken, turning it into a lovely red. I thought of the lovely spotted trout in the burn that I caught with a bent pin. Could it possibly compare with the fish we would catch by the sea, and now available to us? It was possibly wrong to dwell on momentous happenings of the past, raking them up, nostalgic events that did not seem of much importance at the time. I missed the gurgling of the burn I fished in, I missed the smell of the peat and I was still waiting to hear the cuckoo calling, mingling with the bubbling song of the curlews from the meadows

5

down below. I was told to have patience as it was not yet May and we had not gone to a foreign land. The seagulls, squawking as the little fishing smacks came in, did not interest me at the time. I had the chance of more friends if I so wished. But yet again, I was choosy and could not shake off the closeness of those whom I had left behind.

Why did we have to manure the potatoes with seaweed, instead of fertilizer, as we did in the hill croft? It was messy and difficult to carry. To save money I was told. Well, I said, you make extra money on the whelks. But that had to be used for fencing, which we now required to keep neighbouring sheep off our croft. No burn to separate us this time from neighbouring crofts. The fence would be good for shaking the hay up on for it to dry. Extra work I thought, but if this is progress, all well and good.

No cheeky hen to come and say good morning, they were now fenced in a little bit away from the house. Do they miss the closeness they had with us before, as we still had some of our old stock? Even their eggs tasted different, a brighter yolk, which I resented. Why was this? Oh, they scratched and got the sea sand, I was told.

There were some things on the plus side. We had hedgerows teeming with birds' nests, hedges so prickly we could hardly get our hands in. That was the idea of building them there.

Now to look for treasure troves, we had to beach-comb, and a lot more was to be found there. Things thrown overboard, relics off wrecks and plenty of lovely stones to adorn that much wanted garden.

Our small grey cat, whom we managed to flit, (not easy to flit a cat), seemed also at a loss, and started to miaow at the door. When I opened it, she ran towards me, tail held high, crossing and re-crossing in front of me, her flanks heavy with the kittens about to be born, wondering where she would secretly have them this time. She could not make her way back to the old croft, or could she? I gave her some milk which she avidly drank, and afterwards did not know what to do to show her gratitude, again arching her back against my ankles, and even rolling over in my path as if she wanted me to cease my activities to pay attention to her. After all, she was paying me a compliment, and she was not enjoying her new haunts.

I am sure she was also confused by all the different smells, being used to the pipe smoke and the peaty smell, she had the added ones of the salt-laden sea breezes, enfolded with the cooking smell, the most prevalent of these owing itself to the row of kippers. She had got used to the pungent smell of onions, which were always used in the mutton stock, but I think she preferred the aroma of the kippers, as she seemed to hang around the house much more now. How dare she forget those tiny trout I used to throw her, instead of putting them back in the burn! I too prefer the pungent smell of onions.

Now life revolved around the flagpole of religion, everything seemed to be done in the fear of God, not for the love of God, or so it seemed to me. That was the impression we were given. My father had an abiding sense of responsibility to God, and was trained to have a healthy respect for the Almighty, who worked His will in a good Scottish manner, with thunderbolts and threats of hell, fire and wrath to come.

A local thunderstorm was the most terrifying experience of my childhood. Mirrors were covered, windows opened, and everyone was in earnest prayer on their knees asking to be spared, because to us this was God in his wrath.

As we had moved to more civilized parts it meant morning worship, Sunday School in the afternoon, and an evening service. Why do I not know my Bible better than I do?

I cannot recall so may tummy bugs as we have nowadays, despite the fact that I used to go to the butcher slaughterhouse with an old tin pail for blood to make black-puddings. Mother washed the skins in the burn where we played at trying to catch eels and we never suffered as a result. Did germs exist then?

Most daughters whose mothers knew adversity by being born at the wrong time, or in the wrong place, dream of one day repaying a thousandfold for their love and sacrifice. In my case it did not happen. Being headstrong and young, I could not wait to flee the nest, as much as I loved it. My intentions were that I would go out into the big world, make money and buy my mother and father such things as a Tilly lamp and woven carpets, instead of rag-made rugs. Did I do those wonderful things? No, fate caught up with me – I fell in love, and before I could come down from that cloud, the clouds of war emerged and my husband, being a territorial, was into uniform on 3rd September 1939.

Can we go back? No of course we can't, which is just as well. Only a child's mind could cope with the excitement of finding dozens of black tadpoles in a puddle, and in the next puddle what I thought was a rejection of tapioca pudding, later to learn it was frogspawn.

The excitement of my first lick of an ice-cream cone, in the nearest town – I took one bite, not a lick, and yelled: 'I am burnt!' and spat it out on the coconut-matting on the shop floor, much to mother's disgust and annoyance, and that of the lady behind the counter who had to clean it up.

Then the memories of a school cleaner, who was petite, silver-haired and smelled nice and clean. She made sure that our classrooms were also nice and clean. The white, wooden floors were kept clean by the sprinkling of Dusmo and, with a switch brush, were almost scrubbed clean. Glowing bright fires met us on a frosty morning. I would like to know what her annual income was.

We all respected her and yet I never knew her proper name, other than Kirsty. Her haven was a thatched cottage on the brow of the hill above the school, the plastered walls decorated by pages of the *People's Journal* instead of wallpaper, or pages of the *Tatler*, added to the pattern.

Any catastrophe at playtime, such as falling in the school burn and getting your knickers wet, Kirsty's cottage was the refuge, and they soon dried at her peat and twig fire. How did we repay her? Certainly we respected her, but young children can be innocently wicked.

The roads were not fully tarmacadamed in those days but had a good covering of tar. On a hot, sunny day, the tar would melt, so in our bare feet we would stand in it, walk on our heels and then walk in at playtime and leave our tarry footprints on the almost white wooden floor. Can you image Kirsty's feelings next day?

I loved school and will always remember the first day of our new headmaster. He was deeply immersed at his desk, evidently going through our exercise books, hand writing etc, when all of a sudden he slammed down the lid of the desk, caught the lot and threw them on the open fire in disgust, almost putting out the fire. I exploded with laughter, much to the amazement of my class mates. Then, in his Western Isles accent, he said: 'Come out here and I will give you something to laugh about!' Out came the cane, which, I was glad to say, I sampled for the first and last time in my life. Otherwise, I would never have known what it was like, and would not have been able to pity those who got it more regularly.

That was my introduction to Monty, whom I loved to hate, but who was respected by the time I left school, and who made a better scholar of me.

We always had what we termed a 'bare foot race', to see who was the hardiest and first to discard their footwear early in the year. It was always won by a family of four boys, whether by necessity or sheer determination to win, I do not know. March month seemed to be the goal. No prizes given, just admiration or jealousy from the rest of us.

Did cocoa ever taste as good as it did in 1926? No I don't think so, and it never will. Your piece consisted of oat cakes that broke in your bag, and discoloured soda scones, sodden by the black-currant jam. But when you are hungry you eat anything, and I mean when you are really hungry!

I loved sliding and sledging, which we did on a gradient at the back of the school, but it held fear for all!

Each night my father examined the soles of my boots to see how many tacks or studs were missing. One or more was worse than getting a tooth knocked out in a punch up!

I can only recall a doctor being called out once to attend me. I had pinched and eaten enough unripened gooseberries to make a dozen tarts and my parents thought I had appendicitis pains. I only admitted what I had done when the doctor was probing my abdomen. I was ordered to take a large dose of castor oil. Ugh! The cure was worse than the disease, the bed-clothes were saturated with oil before they got enough down my throat.

We cannot compare women of that era with today's. The average woman married, bore children and kept a man happy. She loved her children. In my area their endearments in Gaelic proved that. They grew old gracefully and what was more rewarding than an elderly aunt or grandmother to wipe away tears, or to cool a hot forehead, by laying a loving hand on it, when mother was busy. I'm glad I experienced those kindnesses, as I was able to administer the same in later years. No need for playgroups in those days, Grannies took on the responsibility.

The housewife's morning duty, after stirring up the peaty fire was to put on the girdle for breakfast, or for baking I should say. Can you imagine the lovely aroma for breakfast: hot scones with the golden butter dripping from them, plus crisp oat cakes. Who wanted the cotton-wool loaf? No need for fancy cereals, when treacle from the barrel was slaked on the scones.

Referring back to hygiene, I think all the medicine cupboard held, as I already said, was carbolic soap, maybe epsom salts, castor oil and some bandages made from unmendable clean sheets. A badly cut hand was never stitched but the wound was covered with the biggest black cobweb to be found in a shed and within a couple of days the wound was closed. I could not tell those tales to my grandchildren as I know they would say: 'Rubbish Granny!'

Following outbreaks of measles or scarlet fever, all the rooms were fumigated by burning sulphur on a shovel. The stench would kill any organic thing in sight.

Still on a medical theme, the old people believed that when the leaves appeared on the trees and when they fell, it was time to attend to one's body by swallowing as much sulphur as one could lift on a silver three penny piece, washed down by a treacle drink. Possibly half the tablets we swallow today contain sulphur, I do not know. Suffice to say, I am glad I experienced the two eras. I do not think I would swap one for the other, or would I?

I mentioned earlier that life revolved around the flag pole of religion. My father was a Free Church adherent. Notice I did not say Church 'member'. And that meant we had to attend Church twice daily on

Sunday, no matter what the distance was, depending on where we lived. On one occasion we lived in a croft in the hills four miles from Church, so it was a porridge and egg breakfast, then the four mile hike with a few pandrops in our pockets, leaving home at 10.30 a.m. to be in church by 11.30 a.m.

Sunday morning took in Gaelic and English services. The Gaelic service took longer, possibly because the presenter put forward the line of the psalm, which doubled its length. If we stayed for the English service it meant we would not return for the evening service, but still we were in Church until 2.00 p.m.

The order of the Free Church was that one stood for prayer and sat for singing. The prayers were usually longer than one psalm. The occasional dropping on the floor on a pandrop, relieved the tension. Nobody ever admitted who dropped it, as fear would not allow them.

Communions were the highlight of the year. All kinds of folk arrived, everybody claiming to be a forty-second cousin, or such, and blessing the house, and all in it before they entered. In other words, unpaid guests who could put up a prayer as good as the next man.

They seemed to travel from one sacrament to the other, and all appeared to be really God-fearing men, they could pray as well as any minister. Some of the women guests could put up a prayer as well as the men.

No matter how humble our fare was before communion, the table groaned with food for those four days from Thursday to Monday. The only consolation of sleeping on a shaky down was the extra food and goodies we got when clearing the tables, no tips or extra sweets for the hard work.

Saturday evenings were hectic, all boots polished, all Sunday meals prepared, all fuel brought in, not a dish was washed on Sunday. Can you imagine what Monday was like as the guests departed with another blessing as the only thanks?

So that was the flag pole that our life revolved around. Do what you like Monday to Saturday, then, wham! – Sunday, the guilt overwhelmed one, or it was supposed to. Despite worship being taken twice a day

11

before and after all meals, I could never fathom out whether we were more frightened of God or man.

So, with all the ups and down of life, more ups than downs, that is why, after fifty-one years of marriage and all the modern equipment, I have to hand all the joys and sorrows we acquired, with five daughters and their offspring, and sit and reminisce of the son we never had to help us in our way of farm and croft life that we followed, because like myself, the girls fled to the outside world.

When I think about those two crofts of my childhood, given the chance, which one would I choose? The one in the hills where the blue irises stood like sentinels in the marsh, and the burn went purling over stones below the wooden bridge – Achnahinich.

Chapter 2

The only news of the outside world was the weekly paper received at the weekend. It was sufficient, the luxury of a wireless having not yet arrived. The old fashioned gramophone, the type you wound up, provided enough light relief if there was time to relax. Knowing this you will guess why the 2nd September 1939 and its happenings always meant so much to me; more so than to those who were involved in the full flow of worldly things and events at the time.

The most important thing for me, on 2nd September 1939, was that I was going to a Territorial Dance in the village hall, three miles away from the farm where we lived. Granny was to baby sit. I loved dancing, and this was to be my first dance since my daughter, Ann, was born.

It dawned a lovely sunny day. A super day for drying nappies and so on. As I tripped gaily back and forth to the washing green, I could hear the reaper and George's instructions to the horses as they turned at the end with the rig.

Hubby's tartan trews were pressed and boots polished. I then had a peep in the wardrobe, and looked longingly at the red, satin backless dance dress. No, I wouldn't wear it. I'd wear the wine velvet skirt and the oyster satin blouse. After all, I was a married woman now and couldn't flaunt my figure, as I had the handle of Mrs to my name! Excitement mounting, I skipped over the chores. Baby was sleeping soundly so I decided to 'top and tail' myself, we didn't have a bath in those days. I pinched some of the baby powder, laid out my Ballito silk stockings and gold sandals, and gathered them all to put in a small case which I would place on the pram apron, as I walked the three miles to

13

mother's. George would follow in the evening on his bike.

That afternoon, I was sitting relaxing with the baby on my knee, when George came in, his face white as chalk. I said: 'What's wrong?'.

'Where is my uniform?', he enquired.

'It is all ready' I said. 'I will take it with me, save you carrying it on your bike'.

His expression changed again and he said: 'I need it now, we have to go. Sergeant Anderson is here, Germany has invaded Poland.'

None of this made sense to me. I sat transfixed. If somebody had stepped out of outer-space I wouldn't have been more confused. What had Territorials to do with Poland? All I could relate to the Territorials was that once a year they camped at Barry and he brought me a nice present back on his return.

He hurriedly dressed, came through and kissed us both. I said: 'But where are you going?'.

'Oh,' he said, 'We've got to meet at the Drill Hall.'

'Oh well,' I said. 'See you there, at the dance tonight.'

He gave a very shallow smile and hurried out, where Sergeant Anderson was awaiting him. Suffice to say, there was no dance that night and when I arrived at mother's, still thinking of that night out, it was to find her in tears and looking for something to act as black-out material. In hindsight, she was probably thinking of the last war.

I was more confused than ever, and, after a little explanation, also ended up in tears. Firstly, to think I was going to be deprived of that dance. Secondly, to realise I would not see hubby tonight, or for a long time to come. In my mind I damned the Territorials. If he had not been one he would still be cutting the corn as a farm worker, and would have been exempt from being called up, at twenty-seven years of age. Had it been worthwhile being a Territorial, for six pounds a year? Certainly not, I thought.

Ignorance is bliss, and it served me well for the weeks to come, until the awful truth dawned on me. Where did they go? Had they been spirited away to Poland or what? If I had known they were only forty miles away in the nearest town, installed in a disused distillery, I would

14

have been out with the pram and some goodies. Instead, after two days, I reluctantly headed home over those three, weary miles. The silence and waiting was intolerable. I really felt I must get access to a wireless. If we'd had one we could have been forewarned of the political situation and caused George to have a broken leg or something, anything to prevent the present situation.

I felt I was in limbo until he came home on three days leave, at New Year, before setting off for France. Not that they knew where they were going. I thought, good, they have been to Poland and back.

I made sure I got access to a wireless and used to go to the house of a friend who had newly acquired one. But och, it was no good, as all we heard was that traitor William Joyce, Lord Haw Haw, with crushing news. Anyway, I had my daughter, Ann, and a weekly allowance of 17/6 from the Army and I had the power of prayer. How did I have the time for all those prayers as I normally raced through the Lord's Prayer?

I do not need to waste paper by going into the details of my thoughts at that time. There were thousands in similar circumstances to me. However, I was glad when he eventually came back safe, but not sound, as he was invalided out of the army.

George was in a field hospital in France when, quite suddenly, they were shipped across to England. He was quite ill with stomach and chest trouble. He could not understand why the orderly attending to him in France should also be in the hospital he was admitted to in Kent. George asked him how he came to be there with him? He was told by the orderly that they'd had to make a break for it, from the advancing Germans, and even had to leave the tents behind. The following day came the evacuation of Dunkirk. After a while in hospital, he got home on leave. Eventually, in 1941, he was discharged as being unfit for military duties.

I was quite relieved to hear about the stomach trouble in a sense, because in one of his letters he asked if I could send some baking soda in his next food parcel. Having read in some letters that they slept in barns and pig sties, I had visions of him giving it to some farmer's wife, or daughter, to bake some scones; a commodity possibly they couldn't get. It wasn't all that difficult to conjure up a picture of him giving the soda for scones to bake. So, you see how the green eyed monster creeps in, even at the height of war! When, upon his return, he spoke of how grateful he was for the baking soda to counteract the acid in his stomach, I smiled to myself.

The next harvest my husband cut was a real joy for me. Maybe not to him, because farm wages were only £4.12s a month. But we did have a free house, and milk and hens. And we cut our own firewood.

So, there I was, back to what I'd run away from on the croft by the sea. No Tilly lamps and no woven carpets. What did I abandon between the croft and my marriage? The other side of life, something like 'Up Stairs, Down Stairs'. I had been a maid to an honourable lady and a valet to a future Lord Chamberlain to the Queen. I saw all the carpets, jewellery, and all the pomp and ceremony, but I held it all in disdain. They had all those servants, and the attendance demanded of us, and we were paid with peanuts. Some of their guests we had to attend to left much to be desired. Maybe if I had the luck of ending up as a Lady So and So, I would not have been writing those last few lines!

Anyway, our main priority now was to feed and clothe ourselves. I often sat and laughed at my big ideas. I didn't cry, I was happy and I had good neighbours. George was home though the war was still to be won.

How do you arrive at a suitable diet for a duodenum ulcer? Well, white flesh was recommended, though we had hens we couldn't afford to kill them as they were producing eggs. So it was a case of ordering one weekly, from the butcher, at six shillings (30 pence nowadays) per bird. We had our own milk and eggs, the occasional rabbit that we snared and fish we caught. But six shillings weekly was a big slice cut off a small wage of little more than one pound a week. And, though I did not have children in school, I still had to do my sums every day.

We were all sweet toothed, so sugar was our biggest miss. However the introduction of saccharin helped. The one popped into our cup of tea saved some sugar for baking and milk puddings; much better for one than unsweetened tea. Having had a reserve store of flour and meal, which we used to buy by the boll or hundredweight, meant home baking was very much favoured to the dark loaf we now had to eat.

16

So, all in all, living on the farm had its advantages, plus we could always catch the occasional trout in the nearest river.

The expectancy of another baby meant another ration book. I was hoping to breast feed this one too. However, it would be quite a while before it required the allowance of tea, sugar, butter and cheese, so the three of us were able to share it.

This baby was bound to be a son, to work the horse in years to come, I thought and hoped. It was a home confinement, as before, which meant George hanging about the house; no hubbies were allowed in labour rooms in those days. But the minute he heard the baby's cries, he rushed into the kitchen, grabbed a sweater, jumped on his bike, and rode to the nearest pub, quarter of a mile away. He didn't stay long as he couldn't get any whisky so he came back with a few tots of brandy instead.

By now the doctor was in the kitchen, scrubbing up. George offered him a sip of brandy. The doctor said, 'Well what are you going to call her?'

'Her!' George slurred: 'It's not a boy?'

'No, George, you'll have to try again,' came the doctor's reply. I was disappointed it was another girl. George never voiced his feelings. My mother rebuked me and said, 'Would you prefer to have boys who might end up as gun fodder in the next twenty years?' This made sense to me as the war was still going on. She must have influenced us very much. Is that why we produced another three girls?

I willingly agreed to the family names of Katherine Ann for my first born – Katherine for George's mother, and Ann for my sister, who had recently died. But the selection of 'Sybil', for my second daughter, caused a family furore. Whoever had heard of Sybil? Mother was rendered speechless, suggesting a dozen family names, on either side, to which I listened and said nothing. As the days passed, it was time for George to go and register the baby. With the name sealed in an envelope, he set off on his bike. The registrar opened the envelope. I don't know whether my writing was legible, or, even as a registrar in the Highlands, he had ever heard of the name. He asked, 'What is the name?'

'Annabelle,' said George.

'No, no,' he said. 'I mean the first name.'

'I don't know,' George said.

'Well it spells S-Y-B-I-L. How do you pronounce it?' said the registrar.

'I don't know,' replies George. I am sure he thought, what an uninterested father. George returned and said: 'I thought the baby was to be called Annabelle?'

'She can if she chooses in later life, but in the meantime she is to be Sybil,' I replied.

'Wait till your mother hears of this,' he said. I think mother thought I was the talk of the village. Imagine – Sybil, and all those lovely family names.

There was an ironic sequel to Sybil's christening. The minister, who married us and christened Ann, the Reverend Robertson, was away on active service and so we had to arrange the christening with a replacement minister. However, it so happened that Revd. Robertson came home on leave but the replacement minister didn't mind us asking the Reverend Robertson to christen the baby. We were all very happy at the event, and he felt honoured to be asked, but he did remark: 'That's an unusual name'. I luckily still had a few pieces of wedding cake, very mature, in a tin box. They were the only goodies, the rest of the christening tea being made up of pancakes, scones, egg sandwiches and no drink.

I settled down to a nice quiet life. I had my two little girls, who were company for each other. My girlfriends came on leave, one bringing me a bit of colour in the dark days of the war – a pair of red laces and a pair of blue ones to brighten my walking shoes. Seemingly, they were all the rage down south. The sight of these nearly put my father into a seizure. What was happening to me? A baby called Sybil, and now a married woman with coloured laces. I would be the talk of the locality. Bear in mind he was a Free Church adherent. Poor father, it was a blessing he did not live to see the mini skirt! Oh, those laces did brighten up my life. At the same time, all the tales from the W.A.A.F.S and the A.T.S set me wondering what I had missed out on by being married with a child. I too might have been in the forces. I thought that they were lucky. Oh no, they thought I was the lucky one. Two lovely wee girls and a nice husband, which they still had to find, and I was stuck away in the Highlands, far away from the bombings and the war that was raging.

I read and also wrote a lot during those days, and lived in a world of fantasy and fallacy. It does not cost a lot and it can work wonders at a time when you are busy attending to chicks. They were a must for extra cash and by December I sold my first batch of cockerels, as it was near Christmas. I received a good price, which more than covered the food bill. Cockerels pay, and hens die in debt, so I was to believe. I never examined my hen notebook to check for anticipated profits, to see what I got. Expect four eggs per week, per hen, it stated. As long as we had enough for breakfast, baking, and the odd dozen to the grocer, that suited me.

To rear children on a farm is a lovely, contented life, because anything outside farm life, the village or the town, is a novelty to them, something they appreciated when the occasion arose, which was seldom. There are always comings and going on a farm, and never a dull moment. My husband and I were born into it, so it was more or less inbred into the children. Such were my ideas at the time that I hoped that one or two of them would marry a rich farmer and we could end our days in a nice little farm cottage, rent free. Fantasy again, for nothing could be further from their thoughts. They had possibly seen enough grass and mud.

Life in the west seemed as if it did not belong to the outside world, so, we decided to move further down the country, to Easter-Ross. The farms were bigger, wages a little higher, and there was more of a social life. Troops were billeted all around us. We locals tried to entertain them, by making special teas, dances and concerts for them. Oh, those good looking Norwegian boys, so blonde and so handsome! Fantasy again took over. If father knew of my wicked thoughts, which to him would be equally as bad as deeds, I would certainly be heading down the road to hell. We had Black Watch soldiers, Norwegians, engineers, and the R.A.F., the lot, and all within a ten mile radius, plus the navy at Invergordon. However, we were now within reach of enemy aircraft and good targets they had. So, amongst all the socializing, there was a constant threat. When news came through that the Duke of Kent's plane had come down, we all jumped to the conclusion that it was the enemy, but as the country knows, it was not.

George soon curtailed my dancing with the troops. I was pregnant again. Oh well, it was worth it, to get a son and another ration book. Granny laid down the rules, another girl, if only to make up for all the furore over the name of Sybil. When the baby arrived, I named her Mhairi McKenzie, after Granny, much to her delight. When she got the telegram to say Mhairi had arrived, she caught the first train to come and see this Mhairi and to look after us yet again. In those days, a mother had to stay in bed for up to ten days after giving birth. By now, things were in really short supply, cups could not be replaced, bed linen and soap were also scarce. Granny came with a parcel of white sheets to be cut up for pram and crib sheets. What else did she have? Why, a large tin of soft green soap, which was extremely good for shampoos etc.

Some of the soldiers used to come for fresh eggs to send home. Who can recall the wooden egg boxes suitable for posting? On several occasions, they brought up a large seven pound tin of syrup, (no doubt pinched from the cook house), and some hard biscuits from their iron rations.

We were especially friendly with an English sergeant who came every two weeks for eggs to send home. No doubt his wife sent something nice in the return egg box.

One lovely, sunny day, after a cup of tea, he said he was going to try and find rooms for his wife and two children, so they could come up for a holiday. I suggested he try some of the farm houses. Up until now, we did not have any personal losses in the war but when we heard in the evening that a sergeant was accidentally shot, on his way home from collecting eggs, we quickly jumped to the conclusion that it was an enemy sniper. However, it turned out to be even sadder, when we learnt that our friendly sergeant was shot by one of his own cooks, in jest. As he opened the cook house door, one of the cooks picked up a rifle, and pointing it at him in fun said: 'Hands up, no entrance!' and fired. The gun was loaded. The soldier who had left the rifle loaded was brought to book, but that was no consolation to the sergeant's widow and children.

This tragedy affected us very much, more so than if he had died at the hands of the enemy.

Suddenly, all the troops seemed to leave the area, possibly in readiness for the D-Day landings. No goodbyes, no hints of disappearing. How many returned we would never know. We had the odd land mine dropped in the fields by the enemy. Better to drop them somewhere, anywhere, rather than take them back, perhaps they thought. Possibly the fleet at Invergordon was meant to be the target, or the small airfield seven miles away.

We soon had itchy feet again, so we moved further south to central Scotland. This was an education for us. We were surrounded by prisoner of war camps, full of Italians and Germans, who were sent out to work on the local farms. It was fun trying to teach them English. They were allowed one pass a week from their camps, from 6 p.m. till 10 p.m. so we had them in for an evening. We used to play darts, counting their score in their own language. I used to try and get spaghetti or macaroni for their supper, so that they would feel at home, for which they were grateful. Always amongst a batch of men, for no apparent reason, you became more attached to one or two, over the others. George and I really befriended two of them, and felt sad at the prospect of them returning home one day, but at the same time we felt happy for them. The bond was so strong that, on their last evening, they did not come to the house, but, under cover of darkness, left their only blanket outside our door, and the words: 'Thanks' and 'Love', written on a note. In the morning, we found this note, but could not quite fathom the message. Our cottages were built beside a railway line, and that same day, at 11 a.m. as I was hanging out the washing, I heard a train go by, with its hooter going. I looked up, and there were Cammerite and Dominic, waving from the engine cab. I lay down my washing basket and went in and cried. I told George the story at lunchtime and he also shed a few tears. Neither of us realized they would be repatriated so soon, or did they know? Later, we did have a letter from Cammerite, from an Ayrshire camp they had been sent to before they were fitted out for going home.

So, there again, we were emotionally affected by war. The German prisoners of war were more arrogant and, I think, considered themselves a cut above us. Here again though, from amongst many, there were one or two who were very friendly towards us, and enjoyed the comfort of our home. They made many toys for the children, from wooden match boxes, wire and wool. These were the men against whom George started fighting at the beginning of the war.

Next door to us lived an elderly couple whose son was a German prisoner of war for five years, since the days of Dunkirk. Their emotions were hard to control as peace was signed. They had not heard from their son for a long time and they did not want to raise their hopes too high. Each week I held some meat back to give them, in case he appeared, as they had only two ration books and we had five. They eventually got a telegram as to when he would arrive. His mother made a lovely big pot of soup. I gave her some mince, and she made a rice pudding, none of which poor Bob could do justice to, as his stomach had shrunk after so many years in Stalag Eight. So, a disappointed mother, but a happy Bob.

Now the V.E. Day celebrations were being organized all over the country. I will never forget standing on the streets of Perth as the band of the 51st Highland Division, and the Black Watch Pipe Band, played through the city. We all stood and cried buckets of tears. Tears of joy can be as fast flowing as tears of grief.

Around the farms, we had our celebrations, such as sports and games. I was in the ladies' football team and George was in the men's. I can't remember who won but I certainly remember the following morning – I could hardly crawl out of bed, and I couldn't sit on the toilet. I thought I was paralysed for life and couldn't understand what had happened to me, until George explained that it was my muscles, after playing football. I was in agony for days and never again took that form of exercise.

During the war we could not get home to the west without a passport as our district was designated a security zone. This passport I still have to this day.

Mother and father came on holiday to us at the end of the war, and being a crofter, father was intrigued by the huge farms around us. He had heard of the £15,000 bull, bought by the farmer down the road, and we went especially to see this animal before it went abroad to Argentina. My mother, like myself, imagined a huge, ferocious animal, and could not believe it when a ten month old short horn calf was pointed out to us. Artificial insemination came into the conversation, and boy, did I have a difficult job trying to explain that one! I don't think I ever succeeded.

Our children were now of school age and loved the Broons in the *Sunday Post*. However, no Sunday paper would be read while Granny and Grandpa were there. I produced it on the Monday. My father, who was always a great reader, said: 'Oh, this is a grand paper' and then noticed the name of it: 'Why is it called the Sunday Post?' 'Oh well', I said: 'It is printed after midnight but I suppose they still term it Sunday.' My answer was accepted.

My mother was fascinated by my wall decorations. We could not get wall paper so we emulsioned the walls with two or more colours at hand. We dipped a sponge in them and speckled the walls to make a pattern. She had a ten roomed house at home, so she thought this was a great idea and could not wait to get back home to try that one out.

As I said earlier, our cottages were beside a railway line, so with the open wagons of coal which fired the engine, there were always lots of lumps of coal that fell onto the line. We used to gather these and risk going in between train times. This practice was possibly against the law but we did it all the same. One time my friend and I nearly lost our lives when a goods train arrived unexpectedly and we had to hurl ourselves down a steep embankment. That was the last time we ventured out on that job. All kinds of cooking and heating were dependent on that fire. How quickly you boiled the kettle the 6 a.m. for the first cup of tea before George went to feed the horses.

As the girls grew a little older, there was another way of earning a few extra pennies – by sending them berry picking. They ate as much as they picked to begin with. However, the novelty soon wore off, then it was a race against one another to see who could fill the pail the quickest, and put the pennies in their pockets. The prospect of going to town was an added incentive. The potato harvesting was not so attractive though more money, it was a dirty, back breaking job, and not recommended by their mother, who usually had to finish their stages with cries of: 'Oh, Mum come and help me.'

When the three girls were all at school, there was the yearning for a son. Surely, after four years, our luck would change. I even booked into hospital instead of having a home confinement. It all felt different. We bought a new hood for the pram and ordered a cot. The girls were so excited at the thought of a brother.

The spring of 1947 brought the worst snow in years. I could not even get into the clinic as no buses ran for weeks. Yes, I thought, everything is different. What a glorious hot summer to follow. The 19th of August was unbearably hot, and what did I produce, another girl! I lay there, thinking of George going to a public phone in the morning to be told of yet another girl. I felt a failure, but at the same time enjoyed the attention of the nurses in the ward, and the company of the other mothers, and the good meals. It was a rest. Everything about that pregnancy was different, and the end product has been different from all her sisters. Not in looks, but in personality. I thought I had better use up all the family names, so she became Christine Margaret Elizabeth, now known as plain 'Tina'. Well, she got the choice of that which she preferred.

That was me stuck at the helm for the next five years. You didn't have to go to pick the potatoes or berries if you had a baby, so that suited me fine.

My social life still consisted of dancing classes and W.R.I, a great relaxation away from the children. No television as yet, but there was radio, imparting good general knowledge, stories, plays, and Scottish country dancing music. Political news wasn't of much interest to me then. Some things were still rationed. The only holidays we could manage were those home to the west, and that really was just a change of sink. It was nice to see old faces and compare our children. Mother was a very accomplished knitter and she supplied the children's jerseys, and a good job she did, as I was not a knitter.

Having young girls so close to one another meant they were great company for each other, for fights as well as games. And when mum and dad joined in the fun in a game of rounders at the end of the day, it made the only girl who lived at the big house nearby, quite envious of our collective company and the fun we had at our own back door or yard. The girls valued their father's attention and company and took him out to play with them after a hard day's work. They took mother for granted. Oh no, she couldn't be tired, she only worked in the house, she was her own boss. But poor Dad had to work for a boss. Dad, falling when wearing his tacketty boots, and slipping over a stone was much more fun than mum falling when the buckle on her sandal broke.

It is always said that there is a special bond between a daughter and her father. This I think is true. Could it be, that as a son grows up, there is a jealousy between the father and growing son, whereas girls characterise the wife and mother of males, who in turn, seek to depend upon them.

Now that all the girls were in school, I became more involved in social life, adding drama to my country dancing and W.R.I. activities, being very active in all three. I have been president of the W.R.I, producer of plays, each having its own little moments of crisis if things went wrong in the formations, it was such fun being chastised, as if we were children again.

I baked every day but the highlight of the baking world was when all the Institutes were in competition with one another, twice a year. We were ten Institutes, competing against one another, apart from our own monthly competition. I was still reduced to a coal fire for baking, but later advanced to a Rayburn cooker which had an excellent oven, which in turn meant excellent results. There were very many practices in between competitions so there were always full tins, even if the rest of the cupboards were bare.

In January 1951, I got word that my father was very ill, and was asked to return home. With four young children, it was a big decision to make, but for a few days they would come to no harm, I thought. So George set off with me at 7.30 a.m., in a Landrover, to drive me the thirteen miles to the nearest station. Just as I was leaving Sybil complained of a sore throat. I told her, and the rest of the children, to stay in bed until George returned, which should have been at 9.00 a.m.

The snow was heavy that morning, and became heavier as we travelled to the station. George didn't wait for my train to come in, as he was anxious to get back to the children. It was a long time afterwards, maybe a year, before I heard the story of his hazardous journey home. He did not get back until midday. The icicles were clinging to his hair as he looked out of the window to see where he was on the road, and at the level in the petrol tank. His anxiety for the children must have played tremendously upon his nerves.

Sybil's sore throat produced spots, which our neighbour thought might be scarlet fever. However, the spots cleared up too quickly. I returned from my father's to find Sybil still in bed. Our eldest, Ann, and a neighbour, played down the situation. Nonetheless, I was still worried, and so I called the doctor, only to discover she had rheumatic fever. I nursed her through that; no doubt nowadays she would have been admitted to hospital. Sybil eventually recovered but she was left with a weak valve in her heart.

There was plenty of everything now, still not enough money, but life was good. The girls began to earn some money before they decided on a career. And with that, guess what? Another bun in the oven – I was pregnant again, after a gap of seven years. Well, they said the body changes every seven years, so here goes, I thought. Another pram had to be bought, I resigned as President of the W.R.I., there was no country dancing, and I had to tell the teenage girls that their brother was now on the way. I cannot recall their reaction, if there was any. I began to resent the loss of my freedom but did not openly admit it. At the same time I had an inner excitement, it was sure to be a boy this time. My friends thought it was a huge joke as my first sickly symptoms I put down to a grumbling appendix, and the doctor thought likewise.

The birth was again booked for hospital. I can still see the midwife's face, looking down at me, saying: 'Dare I tell you what it is?' I said: 'If you were lying here as I am, you would not care what it was, as long as you got rid of it.' I had just produced a 9½lb girl. This was at about 2 a.m. The midwife said: 'Do you think I should phone your husband?' 'No,' I said: 'Let the poor devil sleep till the morning.' She phoned him

26

at 7 a.m. He ran down the stairs, and the globe fell off the lamp, plunging him in darkness, I believe. I never found out what he did say at the end of the phone. I could hardly throw her in the Tay, so I brought her home and gave her the name of Shelagh. I must add that I was depressed for weeks at the disappointment the child was not a boy. Our boss said: 'Can you imagine what a spoilt little brat he would have been with four sisters!' That made sense. I am happy to say she is now the dearest to us, with two lovely boys, and we see her daily.

Well that was me, more or less house-bound again, with just the household chores to satisfy me. The girls were a help with the baby and Christine thought this was a super doll. However, the years rolled by too quickly.

We country folk think townies are so smart in comparison – maybe they are in fashion, but not in the three R's they are not. I had a very smart nephew in London who loved to come to the farms we were on, as he enjoyed fishing. His first visit as an adult was nearly his last. Going to bed very late, after a good sing song, or ceilidh as we call it, I put a lamp in each bedroom – the first time he required a lamp on holiday. I was just falling to sleep when I heard the cries: 'Oh Mary, I'm burnt!'. And there he was on the landing, holding onto the funnel of the lamp, which he lifted off to blow out the wick. I was in hysterics. It took me several seconds to say: 'Drop it', and then I rushed to get medication to soothe his burnt fingers. He may have been around the world in a banana boat, but he certainly didn't know how to put out an oil lamp.

All our country and town friends and relations made yearly visits to us to whatever farm we were on, not only for a cheap holiday, but for an interesting one. Fishermen, climbers, naturalists, all found our home a haven. What would I have given for the present day video in those days. No 'Carry On' film could equal the summer evening, when that same nephew, and my husband, went fishing on the flats in full gear – waders, rods, worms etc. I said, 'I hope you're not going to be eaten alive by the midges.' As they reached mid stream, they noticed the bull from across the river, coming over to charge them. Can you imagine a Londoner knowing how to handle the situation? He dropped the rod, and with waders on, tried to run up through the stubble field, one cow on heat, running to meet the bull; she was the attraction, not the fishers. Though they could have been gored to death, the girls and I couldn't do anything to help for laughing as the cries of 'help!' reached us. How often that tale has been told, I have no idea. Each year, as friends and guests arrived, there was an hilarious incident to relate at a later date. How true they were, yet so hard to believe; and all boiled down to innocence and ignorance on somebody's part.

As the years rolled by, I seemed to be always the hostess, no holiday for me. In my world of fantasy and fallacy, I would read and dream about the bulb-filled fields in Holland, the Costa Brava and the Grand Canaries – all new holiday venues. London was not the beginning and the end of the world, and I had not even reached there by then. As a young girl, I did dream of Australia, but now that was well buried.

Each year one of the girls flew the nest and entered their own vocation. It was the time of the swinging sixties. A whole new world, fashions changed so rapidly. Poor Mum's wardrobe looked so drab. There was the beehive hairdo, stiletto heels which played havoc with the linoleum, and left as many holes, as if a gun had peppered the floor. I looked at my spreading figure and thought it would be lovely to wear those clothes and to afford them. But with suet and steam puddings, sugar, cream and cakes, there was little hope of ever pinching them off the girls.

With the rooms vacant and the girls away I decided on another form of earning money at home. I advertised through the Farm Holiday Guide, and thus began a very interesting stage of my life, taking in paying guests from all walks of life, some of whom proved to be life-long friends, by correspondence and occasional visits. This was a good way to add to the income and still cope with the upbringing of Shelagh, and all the household chores. We still did not have electricity, but calor gas helped with the cooking. Still no washing machines, so sheets were washed by hand and dried outside. Ironing them really was demanding work. No doubt the guests, especially from the towns, thought the coal and log fires, and lamps were novelties. However, the extra money made up for all the extra work.

28

Eating habits were different in those years. There was plenty of everything after the war and nobody thought of slimming. Everybody wanted a full breakfast, full lunch, high tea and supper. Lunch time snacks were not even heard of. There had to be more varied baking to put on the table for the paying guests at high tea. On Tuesday you did not put the same on the table as Monday, otherwise they thought it was leftovers. You could alter the sponge by adding fresh raspberries and cream for the second day. We always had plenty of cream. We now managed the farm, so we had a large farmhouse, plenty of eggs, cream, fruit bushes etc.

My little kitty was mounting up, so now there was time for a holiday. George, Shelagh and I went to London, and saw all the sights: St Paul's, Westminster, Heathrow, Madam Tussaud's, Buckingham Palace, Harrods, Kew Gardens. The shops did not impress me as they all seemed to be the same as we saw in Glasgow or Perth, and the litter on the streets shocked me after the green grass of home. I was glad we did the trip but it did not unsettle me. I had never experienced such queues, and there seemed to be queues for everything. We queued for an hour to get into the Black and White Minstrel Show. I thought about what we could have accomplished in an hour at home, there we seemed to require every minute of every hour.

We were on our own, on a little farm now, and we had to have a different outlook on things. No son to drive the tractor, not even a daughter. So apart from working inside, as well as having summer guests, I was working outside, but I loved it all. Having good neighbours was an added bonus, and Morag, my neighbour, and I, got on well together and shared everything.

Katherine Ann was now training as a nurse in Inverness. She was tall and strong, and would have been a great help on the farm. She came home to celebrate her twenty-first birthday. It turned out to be the equivalent of a wedding. The celebrations could be heard three miles away, in the village. The 12th January 1960 was a frosty night, and the music, singing and dancing, which ended up in the lawn, drifted down the loch side. The guests said, 'Well, if this is her birthday, I'll look

29

forward to her wedding!'

We now rose to the level of tilly lamps and carpets, and more household changes. All the rooms were given new names, the big kitchen became the living room, or dining room, the scullery became the kitchen, and the sitting room was now the lounge. I always meant to order George to take off his muddy boots at the door, but thought better of it. I think I read too many glossy magazines. With no electricity, I had no hoover to do the carpets but acquired a Ewbank sweeper.

Chapter 3

In every village, and Kinloch Rannoch was no exception, there are what we call characters, or worthies. There were three memorable such people in our village in the 1950s and 1960s. They were the Minister, the Doctor and the Domini, (school master), or 'Schooley' as we called him.

Each lacked partners as hostesses, the doctor was widowed, the Domini a bachelor, and the Minister's wife was housebound. At least I never saw her, but I certainly heard her. On the two occasions I had reason to phone the manse, such a booming voice came over the phone, it nearly ruptured my ear drum! I wondered who it was, as I had visions of his wife being very frail as she never came out.

The Minister did not resemble a minister in any way. I maintained his greasy hat would make a good plate of soup, and I felt sorry for him with no domestic help. A very intelligent man, he would have fared better as a lawyer than his chosen vocation. Any information, given or sought, would be strictly confidential. He had an enormous appetite. I recall him visiting one day as I was standing baking pancakes on the girdle. He sat at the end of the table and helped himself as I laid them out on the wire tray, at the same time imparting a lot of knowledge. People do not usually talk while eating a mouthful of hot pancakes but he managed to do so. All quite revolting. On completing my baking, I said, 'Do you have time for a cup of tea?' 'Yes' he said. So I produced a dish of raspberry jam and he dunked a few more in his tea.

You may say I am exaggerating if I were to tell you how many he scoffed altogether but I swear that he ate at least ten raspberry tartlets at Shelagh's christening, aside from anything else! And that was over a period of two hours! The christening was in the house, and as we all sat and chatted afterwards, his hands stretched over several times for yet another tart.

The doctor reminded me of Harry Lauder. For the most part he wore the kilt. He had such a beaming smile, and was a lovely old gentleman. He was very clever with the knife, from lancing a painful gum boil, to a leg amputation. Possibly a medical officer who had seen the battle of Gallipoli had to be.

I had quite a lot of confidence in him till the day he visited George who was quite ill with bronchitis. I climbed the stairs to hear the verdict, only to discover the doctor smoking, and in the process of handing one to George. I had already threatened all sorts of punishment if I ever saw a cigarette in his mouth again, after all his coughing and wheezing. I gave vent to my wrath, only for the doctor to say: 'Och well, he looked so miserable lying there in bed. I thought he needed cheering up!'

As for the Domini, if you had one ounce of brains at all, he made sure he required two or three ounces, and never gave up until he discovered you did not have any in the first place. He was the one whom pupils loved to hate and yet they all invited him to their weddings. Why? Not for the gift, but to hear all the praise he bestowed upon them!

He was a great organiser of village functions. We were all sad that he did not have that supporting partner in life, and sorry at his passing so soon after retirement.

It was hard to replace such kenspeckle (conspicuous) figures in a small community, without there being criticism of their successors.

To return to life on the croft we called 'Carrie'. It was an exciting life, though a tiresome one. George worked for the Forestry Commission, our holding being rented from them.

Weather conditions were a major issue. With quite a promising morning one would think, 'Oh well, I'll stay at home today and start the hay cutting.' Only to discover that by mid-day the rain had come down so hard that a day's pay was lost by not being able to go on to the hill or cut the hay. Such were the many frustrating days I counted during hay making, harvesting and potato picking. I was always trying to cope with two jobs. I coped with the domestic crises, (and there were many), one of which I will make reference to. I was delighted to be able to buy one hundred point of lay pullets, but within a week I noticed one of them had drooping wings. I initially blamed either Shelagh or William, or next door neighbour's little boy, for hitting it with a stone or stick, which they strenuously denied. Soon another one appeared to have the same defect. Again I thought it must have been the children, and compared with the end results, I wished it had been! My whole flock was infected with fowl pest. It meant I had to get rid of them all, and, worse still, I could not rear any more on that ground for five years. The poultry dealers would only cough up one hundred day old chicks as compensation.

As I mentioned earlier, I once brought up the subject of artificial insemination with my Mother, when we were looking at a 15,000 guinea bull calf at the market, and I tried to explain to her that one did not really require one's own bull for the stock. Now the practice came into regular operation in our own small world. One day I happened to notice the signs of a cow in season while George was away planting trees on the hill. I raced on my bicycle to the nearest phone box to phone the artificial insemination man, sixty miles away, and I hoped he would arrive in time. Mother and Father were gone by now so I could do no more explaining to them. The end products were good quality calves, of our own choice, either Short Horn or Aberdeen Angus. There is no way I would have considered midwifery as a career, and yet, being a midwife in the byre did not bother me. Necessity is the mother of invention, and so it was with me, helping to deliver my first calf, with George away at the final of a football match, and only the help of a teenage boy.

I still did not like the idea of milking and did not do it, except in a crisis. The cows seemed to sense my nervousness, and did not willingly part with their milk. Surely my gentle hands must feel better than George's rough ones? Evidently not.

To pail feed a calf takes a wonderful knack and yards of patience. The natural movement of a calf is to butt his mother's flanks when looking for the teat. It does the same to a pail, so you put your finger in the pail for it to begin to suck, and then playfully comes the butt, with the milk splashing all over you. So you try and try again. Having weaned five children, I knew what to do. I had the patience to encourage the calf to drink out of the pail until it became habit forming.

I was quite content to stay on that croft forever, though it was hard work for us both, especially for George, who also had to work for the Forestry Commission – draining, planting and getting many soakings out on the hills where there wasn't any shelter. This contributed still further to his chest complaints, and, after a London holiday where he contracted nephritis, (inflammation of the kidney), it put an end to our life on the croft forever. We had to sit down and study what was to be the next step in our lives. We had to consider the two girls still at school.

Having been used to farm life we could not see past it, so in the end George decided to work as a grieve (foreman) on an out-farm near Dundee. An out-farm meaning that the farmer owned two farms, managing one himself and letting his grieve work the other. Some people would imagine that living on a farm so near to a city like Dundee would be a great advantage, having the best of both worlds. Unfortunately, it did not work out like that for us. We all missed the hills, and to the children, a country school is not the same as that of a town. All-in-all, none of us was happy. I threw myself into a social life, WRI and dramatics classes etc, but it did not make things any easier.

We now had electricity so one of the first things we acquired was a television set. 'The One O'Clock Gang' at lunchtime was the highlight of the day. I had time to watch it now there were no young children to attend, sticks to saw, or butter to make. I felt myself becoming a lazy housewife. Even people living on the outskirts of a city are still city dwellers in their habits and dress sense too. Possibly they looked down on frumpily dressed country folk like ourselves, with our sensible walking shoes and the tweeds we wore in those days. Dress sense did separate people at that time. So you could say we felt a sense of not belonging.

Living so close to the city was convenient in many ways, but unless you had plenty of money to shop with you could become quite lonely in an afternoon. You did not speak to people in the street. No, I was lost for the company of the country. There were two marriages in the offing, and

I could not visualise them taking place in our present surroundings.

I was very unsettled and my mood was rubbing off on George, who seemed quite content with his work, and, being a keen Dundee football supporter, it suited him to live just a few miles away from Dens Park, the home of Dundee football club. But if you do not live with a football team, you have to live with a wife, and a discontented one at that! One who was just waiting to strike while the iron was hot. The opportunity did not arise for eighteen months, and when it did I was ready to pounce.

I had heard of a vacant cottage back in Kinloch Rannoch where we came from. How many would be after that one I asked myself? I had to pull several strings to obtain it, as it was not a council house. It was an advantage that in former years George had worked for the laird, the owner of the cottage. So we were given the tenancy, and the cottage went on to become the centre of all gladness and sadness as the years passed, and the rock that three generations love to come and visit – just a humble little cottage with bulging walls. As the family has grown, it has become unsuitable now, but so many people have come and gone over our doorstep, that I would not change it for a mansion house.

I was back in the village and surroundings I loved, scenery-wise if nothing else, in the lifestyle I was happy with. George did not have permanent work. Farming was out, so I had to help with finances. I went back to the bed and breakfasts, and summer visitors which I always thought was an interesting life, meeting all kinds of people. Some visitors returned who used to come and stay on the farm. The whole family was pleased we were back to our familiar haunts.

I was now back into the swing of the country social life. Shelagh was at secondary school. I was very much a free agent and not tied by animals, other than Corrie our collie dog, who was not very happy being restricted to a house on the street, with no fields to roam around in. In any case we were not even supposed to have a dog in our new cottage. Eventually, we gave her to a shepherd in another area. For months I suffered a guilty conscience for parting with her.

When we got this cottage, the solicitor of the laird, who knew us personally, said, 'Do you think it will be big enough?' 'Oh yes,' I said,

'There are only the two of us and Shelagh, and the others are away working.' I did not take into consideration that being engaged in those days did not mean sharing the same bed, as they do in the 1990s. So, when they did come home, space was very limited.

By now there were three weddings in the pipeline and it was comforting to know that if I could not afford to ask all the locals to the first, they would get a chance at the second, or the third. So that was good thinking in advance, and that is the way it worked out. It meant many had to travel a long way, from such far-flung places as London and Wales. The atmosphere at the first wedding was so good, it lent fire to the prospect of the next, and so on.

Mhairi was the first to marry, and where did she go to live? As far away as London. Little chance of popping in for a cup of tea. We had hardly got over the excitement and emotion of parting with her, when Ann decided to follow suit and before the year was out, she also gave up the state of single blessedness. And where did she go to live? London. As if there were not enough people in London already! Well, there was at least a chance of a holiday down there for us. Now, with two marriages within a few months, what was looming now was a different threat altogether.

I now realised that marriage was the biggest gamble of all in life. You entrusted your happiness, peace of mind, financial security and well-being, to another person. You cannot lecture on all those points to young people in love. I considered myself lucky in having such a caring husband who had never opened a pay packet since we married, but handed it directly to me. No doubt he realised I could possibly make it go further than he could, but at the same time, he must have trusted me from the beginning to do the best I could with it. All I wished for was that my daughters' husbands would be even half as good as their father. I had five healthy girls, but I was not so confident that they would be lucky enough to be mothers with healthy children. I was old fashioned enough to realise the risk of pregnancy. Giving birth can be fraught with danger, not the least of which is the fear of having a physically or mentally handicapped child. So, for years I worried about them growing

36

up, and as they settled down, the worry began all over again, coupled I should add, with the excitement of being grandparents, which was really terrific.

Our cup was overflowing with joy when the first arrived. A grandson, Edward, a real boy after all those girls. With Colin's arrival we could have jumped over the moon. This was really too good to be true. Colin was the name I would have chosen if I had had a son. So, without giving any secrets away, he is special to me amongst all of the offspring.

Marriages, birth and christenings are such happy events to bring the family together, and also food for thought on a dull evening – one's life is never dull again.

Being a mother, the mind has many wavelengths, but being a granny has many, many more. You are always thinking of that innocent bundle and hoping it is managing all right. I could well recall the tiredness of being a mother that those endless sleepless nights bring on, no matter how good the father, he needs his night's sleep to work the next day. So, you see, being a granny means you live it all over again – in your mind. Possibly it is a good thing that my daughters and grandchildren were many miles away, otherwise I could well have been accused of spoiling them.

Having no telephone meant any useful hints were only passed on by letter. I could never tell whether they took any notice of them or not, that's possibly the best way.

My geographical knowledge increased with the arrival of my grandchildren. I would never have seen Epsom Racecourse if Mhairi and her husband Eddie had not lived nearby at Morden. Possibly, I would never have been to Chessington Zoo if Colin had not been born in the same part of London.

What was that tree doing inside the flat Ann and Rhae lived in? To help the cats scratch as they were not allowed out. To somebody living and brought up in the country, that was the funniest thing of all, to see a tree inside a house! They had rented a flat from a couple who had gone to America. You pressed a button in a unit and your bed came down. You pressed another and the television came out, another you pressed in the sink and your rubbish disappeared. I thought I was in Hollywood. This was right up my street, a whole room full of books, I wished I was there for a year! I forgot George was toiling at home. This was good, there were babies appearing all over the place.

Now Sybil thought she would do likewise. Could she not just delay it a little while until we got used to our present set of circumstances, and could gather some more pennies? Oh no, she must get in on the act too.

How can a mother wear the same hat and suit to the third wedding in less than two years? She can't. The men usually just change their ties or shirts. The weddings took place in spring, summer and autumn, so there had to be a change, not that I minded of course!

Where did Sybil go and live after her wedding? Edinburgh – not too far for me to go if another grandchild arrived. But I did have some qualms about this move, due to the rheumatic fever she had as a child. I hoped she would be a mother, and secretly hoped that if so, it would be a girl.

By now Ann had produced twin boys, born prematurely. Mhairi was also expecting a month after Sybil. I thought surely a girl between them must be on the cards. Mhairi pipped her at the post and produced a son, Jason, on the 4th of August, and Sybil's Fiona appeared on the 6th. All those boys were becoming a habit, so wee Fiona was most welcome. Visions of frilly dresses and pants were on the horizon!

I had assumed the role of grandmother to such an extent now that I donned a pair of flat shoes and a pinny. I had to prepare a rota for who was coming and when. With none of the grandchildren at school age they could come at any time and did not have to consider the school holidays.

Coal fires must have been non-existent in their homes, as all the grandchildren were fascinated by the fire, and even more willing to examine it with their hands. So the term 'no touch', with a certain emphasis, deterred them from getting burnt. But anything and everything was apt to be thrown in. Why? Because they saw their elders throw things in the fire, such as wet papers and cigarette ends. Inevitably, some slippers almost suffered the same fate, until I acquired a fireguard once more.

With Christine a few years younger there was a lull in the production. She joined the W.R.N.S, and moved south, and, need I say it, landed in London, after a term in Wales. London must be a wonderful place. However, her description of Whitehall did not appeal to me. The cockroaches seemed rife in that building. She said she was in 'communications' which I could hardly believe, as nobody could understand a word of what she said, with the rate of her delivery. I think she had visions of travelling abroad to far away places. But what did she do? Married, like the rest of them, and eventually left the services when her eldest son David was born. Another boy you will note. Anyway, Sybil's second daughter Anne-Marie, appeared before then to balance things up a bit, and be a playmate for her sister Fiona.

Shelagh, as a very young girl, must have felt ancient with all those nephews and nieces. 'All those boys, Mum', she said. But anyway, Lyn, Ann's youngest, appeared to relieve things. Eventually I hoped Christine and Shelagh might balance things still further by producing girls.

I should not differentiate between them all. They were such lovely, healthy grandchildren, and Grandpa was so delighted with them all, as he loved all babies, whether related or not, and still did in his old age.

We were able to visit them all in their own homes, and saw them growing up in their own environments. Colin, Alan and Ian were like triplets. I thought, what a battle Lyn will have to fight her ground amongst the sand the builders were using to build the houses on the new estate that was going up around them. The builders were very good to let the children play in the sand on their building site, and thank goodness they did give them that freedom, not knowing the devastating news that was waiting around the corner the following year.

Following a medical examination for a trivial complaint, it was disclosed to their parents that their children had Muscular Dystrophy, an incurable muscle wasting disease. This had to be explained to me, as I had never heard of it, and as the reality and full implications of their condition began to sink in, I am sure it destroyed a part of my heart that has never healed to this day. I could not imagine that those three rascals squirming in the mud and sand, could eventually be reduced to wheelchairs. But sad though it is to day, as I write this, it is the case, all except Alan, one of the twins, who is still able to walk.

So, while the outside world sees me laughing, on the inside I am not. Throughout the years George and I think of them daily, and the wonderful task their parents have performed keeping them in their own home, as they wished, no medal could be minted suitable enough to give them, their parents and the courage of Colin, Alan, Ian and Lyn to cope with their disability.

We have had more fun and rapport with that set of grandchildren than with all the others put together. I wonder, are they given a special gift to recompense for their disability? No four children have ever had such genuine grandparents' prayers. We love their visits, but, at the same time, visually it hurts to see them chair-bound. Upstanding they would have been so handsome – as all our grandchildren are. We have enough faith not to question, 'Why them and not the rest of the grandchildren?' I always understood that the healthiest and the most able bodies ones are also vulnerable in life, and this has been brought home to me as my life has progressed.

The news of the Welsh children's disability sent shudders through the other girls and sent them scurrying for tests. But on the surface things seemed to be all right. Soon Lyn, Fiona and Anne-Marie had Paula to support their female line. Edward and Jason loved their little sister. She was so fair and fragile, like a china doll. Oh what a breather from all those babies! But how could I, who produced five, advise them to stop? I did venture to but I did not have much of a respite. Sybil soon produced a boy, Graham.

It was certainly time now to buy a birthday book, nobody could remember all those birthdays. Thank goodness Shelagh was several years younger and not yet of a marrying age.

Yes, I was becoming well 'grannied'. A close look in the mirror, yes there were a few grey hairs there, and the tired legs, and the bad back. I was reduced to bed for a few weeks with a slipped disc, and, at the same time, George was ill with bronchitis. Where were all the girls to help us now? All occupied with families, and Shelagh was away doing her apprenticeship in hairdressing.

However, Tina did come home with David to help us. I could not possibly walk to sit on the toilet, so one morning David's potty was handy as I tried to stand beside the bed. I was in the middle of this performance as Tina was hanging out the washing, when suddenly David says: 'No Granny, David's potty!', he grabbed the utensil and there and then the carpet had a very unexpected shampoo, with yells of help from me! It was a case of I have started so I must finish! Shrieks of laughter from Tina, yells of pain from me.

Chapter 4

There are many who imagine that because we live in the country we must hardly see a living soul. How wrong they are. People come from all the 'airts and pairts', not just family and friends. As we are centrally situated in the village, we get all kinds of people seeking information, from local history and the locations of their ancestors, to sights of local beauty spots and so on.

I am very interested in local history, being a member of a history class. I am always able to give lots of information. There are many Americans of the Robertson clan who maintain their forefathers came from this district. They arrive by bus, with one hour to spare before continuing on their journey. They appear to think they can gain enough knowledge in an hour. They naturally make for the local hotel, meaning to obtain information over a drink, only to find out the hotel is manned by 'foreigners', as they say to me, the 'foreigners' being New Zealanders, Australians and the English. I ask, 'Who do you think you are with your American accents?' 'Oh my grandfather or grandmother emigrated from this district,' they reply.

'Oh well,' I say, 'Possibly all 'foreigner's' forebears did likewise, and that is why they decided to come back and work here.'

Thankfully, I am usually able to give them a lot of information in a short space of time, but naturally there is little time for them to visit all the spots that they would like to.

The mountain Schiehallion, that overlooks, or should I say dominates the village, is such a notable landmark that many people come here to climb it, if for nothing else. Many ask me the nearest route to the summit. Without revealing I have never climbed it, I do my best to impart what knowledge I have managed to pinch from others.

I have already mentioned that I used to do bed and breakfasts for summer visitors, and naturally, you may ask as to why they come to Kinloch Rannoch? Two couples arrived from the Midlands once, and I asked them the same question. They replied that they were divers and had come to see if they could locate the wreck of a steamship that sunk in Loch Rannoch ninety years ago. I could hardly swallow this story until we were deep in the conversation and I found out how they came to know about it, and how they hoped to raise it after such a long time. They were equally amazed that I was not aware of its existence, and that it was not the main topic of conversation amongst the locals. 'Well,' I said, 'Those that knew about it are all gone, and to those that remain, it cannot mean much.'

This, to me, was very exciting bed and breakfasts, but I swallowed their story with a pinch of salt. When I realised the husbands were the divers and their wives the time-keepers, for timing how long they could remain under water, I tried to impress upon them how cold a freshwater loch was, and how dark and murky it would be, with its peaty foundation. I am sure they were all aware of this, but they took it as valuable information.

It was an exciting week, each day producing new results, and ultimately they came up with the proof that they were on to the wreck of the steamship, *Gitana*. They brought back a brass candlestick, and, on taking off the cap, we sliced the top of the tallow and lit it. My neighbour and I had our photographs taken with it.

We were now more than interested in the *Gitana* having had its locaters staying with us. I could write a book about the raising of the *Gitana*, and the success and the heartbreak it brought over the succeeding seven years. But that is history now, and I would like to leave it to others to write about.

Meanwhile there were highs and lows in my own life. I now realised I was to be bothered by a bad back at intervals, if I did not take care of my movements. I did not consider going to an osteopath, or probably thought

I could not afford to. On reflection I now realise how wrong I was on both counts.

It is easier to enjoy the country if you do not have to make a living from it, or so some people think, but I myself do not share that view. Working on the land is a great challenge, and you do reap the rewards. We are now reduced to a patch of washing green and a border of flowers, there is no challenge there and I envy those with a nice garden. I would welcome even the facilities to have three hens, but animals of any kind really tie one to the home, be it a mere goldfish.

Where did I get the love of the land from? Why, my forefathers. They had farming backgrounds for generations, especially amongst the hills. But with the conditions at the time, coupled with added health problems, we both realised we had to say goodbye to that way of life. That is why, in a sense, we felt restricted living on a street, and an inevitable amount of boredom set in. Especially on the likes of a spring and summer evening, for now we did not have to struggle with nature.

Instead of discarding his muddy boots at the end of the day, George had to make sure he had his shoes highly polished, and his bow tie set at the proper angle. What for? Believe it or not, he exchanged his occupation from outdoor to indoor. Hotel work of all things – what a challenge! However, he took to it like a duck to water, the secret being that he was always highly domesticated and was as good working inside as out; a perfectionist in all his work. Everybody had a little smirk on their faces when discussing his latest venture, but he loved it.

I also took up work with a Glasgow corporation at an outdoor centre, at Faskely near Pitlochry. We were now both earning more than we ever did. So, now for the fantasy and fallacies to come true! Tenerife here we come!

George had qualms about flying, but after much coaxing and a few whiskies in the departure lounge, he had enough Dutch courage. However, soon after taxiing down the runway, the plane suddenly stopped. We did not know why and sat and waited patiently. Eventually, after some time, we took off. By this time the effects of the whisky were wearing off, and as we rose in the air, George said. 'That does not sound very good.' I said, 'What do you mean? What would you know if it were right or wrong?' A voice from behind us said, 'You are right, it does not sound right, and I fly every month!' The voice turned out to be that of an ex-pilot. Then a message from the captain came over the public address: 'We can only fly at x number of thousand feet, and have to land at Luton.' It turned out that one of the engines had packed in. So, down we came down at Luton, and we sat on the tarmac for what appeared to be hours. We were still at Luton when we should have been at Tenerife!

It being December, I had travelled to the airport in my winter boots and changed to sandals ready for the sunshine. We were not allowed to leave the plane. However, the doors were opened for the crew to have access which meant my feet became frozen. The hostesses were arguing that they were not going to continue on that flight and made other arrangements for their return, possibly a date they did not want to break.

The mechanics, in their white overalls, worked for hours swotting up their manuals. George, gasping for a cup of tea, or another whisky, which was not allowed while we were here in the UK. At the duty free shop in Glasgow, as I bought some whisky, the assistant said to me, 'Why are you buying it here, I thought you said you are going to Tenerife, it is a duty free island?' Well, being an unseasoned traveller, I could not grasp that message, and duly paid for the whisky.

During the hours we sat at Luton we should have scoffed some of it but being raw recruits to travel, we did not think of getting our bag out and swigging out of a bottle. Four men who came off an oil rig and were going on holiday, were not too embarrassed to do the same thing. Lacking patience at the delay, and not allowed off the plane, they scoffed all they bought at the airport. When eventually we did get going and left the UK, the hostesses went round with the trolley, only to find their path blocked by the bodies of two of the oil riggers – out for the count in the passageway! One of the hostesses went for the captain who tried to rouse them, but with little success. They were dragged to where I do not know, other than they were not thrown off the plane. The plane was full and their other two pals were out for the count in a not too comfortable position, but at least their seat belts were containing them. As we were descending into Tenerife, a message came from the captain concerning the wind direction and the mention of drizzle. That sank my spirits lower than ever. We left snow and now we land in rain! It was so dark we could not see a thing on the hour's bus journey to the hotel, with the exception of the lights of a little town as we passed.

Boy, wasn't I glad to get the key of that bedroom! I collapsed on the bed and left the cases lie until morning. I said to George, 'Will you listen to that storm?' 'I would rather listen to the kettle singing,' he replied, as he looked at the bowl of fruit and a bottle of wine in the bedroom. That wind really shattered me but somehow I managed to gather my wits, and made my way downstairs, where, in my best pigeon Spanish, managed to arrive at a pot of tea, such as it was, and milk of some kind. I discovered later that there were no cows on Tenerife. After a few sips, off came the sandals, off came George's shoes, and not much else, and then we were both out for the count.

I woke early the next morning to the sound of that blinking storm. I rose and drew back the curtains. It was a lovely, sunny day, and the storm that woke me turned out to be waves crashing on the rocks on which the hotel was built. As my eyes got used to the scene, there appeared to be miles of black sand. I woke George, more or less dragged him to the window, and said: 'It is not a storm, it is just the waves crashing on the rocks below and look at the sun, and no sign of rain.' It did not look as though they had seen rain in years.

We were really starving by now and hurriedly dressed. I remembered seeing the Scottish oil rig workers that were drunk on the plane, staggering off only to be picked up by the Spanish police, and I wondered whether the poor things would be getting a drink of tea this morning, and the nature of their fate. They were not in a fit state to even pick up their luggage!

As we entered the dining room, we thought, when on earth are we going to be served? There seemed to be hundreds of people in there already. The restaurant manager directed us to a table, another waiter came to offer us tea or coffee, and we sat and watched. We then realised that we had to go and help ourselves. So we joined a queue to collect a very hard roll, cereal or juice, cold meats or a very cold, hard-boiled egg. I think George was ready for sausage, bacon and eggs, but it was a case of when in Rome do as the Romans do. 'No toast,' says George. I said, 'They will be hard pushed to make toast for this crowd.' He tried to chew that hard roll, with his falsies nearly getting embedded in them. I could not eat for laughing. 'Oh dear, two weeks of this and I will easily get into my bikini!' I thought to myself.

We could not wait to get out in the sun, and investigate this black sand which we thought would make us dirty. It did not, and it was as fine as caster sugar. We were to learn later that we were on a volcanic island.

I was undecided as to whether I had the courage to wear a bikini, even though nobody there knew me personally. However, after sitting a whole afternoon on the beach, I had no hesitation as I watched those big German women jumping in and out of the water. Such pounds of uncontrollable flab I had never seen before. Why they bothered to cover up anything at all I do not know. Their relaxed birthday suits would have looked a lot better than the restriction of some naughty parts. George was disgusted. Anyway, it was good for stimulating the brain, watching all the breeds and creeds at the other side of the world, compared to counting the chickens at home, which looked all the same.

The only thing about the island that was better than where we came from, was the weather. The land was really parched and dry. They had to irrigate all over the island, with water tankers. The water tasted horrible, you could not drink it, and soft drinks were expensive. The whisky was cheap, however, and no wonder, for who could drink whisky in temperatures of eighty and ninety degrees fahrenheit?

George was yearning for a traditional Scottish or British breakfast. We managed to find one at an outside café but when he saw the egg being fried, on what we would have described as a hot plate, and squashed like a pancake, it turned him completely off the idea. The bacon was half raw, and the toast was equivalent to half fried bread. He realised he was as well having a continental breakfast in the hotel. The lunch and the dinner made up for the lack of a fried breakfast, not that we knew what we were eating half of the time. What we thought were a couple of slices of white mealy pudding, though a bit tougher, turned out to be octopus, when we asked the waiter. It was fun finding out what we were having. George really missed his puddings. Sweets were served and there was always fruit – apple, orange or banana.

The restaurant manager always made sure we sat at different tables each day, which was good. We met different people and, if we did not care for them we did not have to put up with them for long. We made many friends, and after all these years, we still correspond with them.

After ten days of inactivity, following a tour of the island, I was ready to be back home with a duster in my hand. A life of luxury did not suit me.

We also spent Christmas and New Year in Tenerife, but for me it is far too nostalgic a time to be away from home. When I phoned my daughters on Christmas Day they seemed very emotional, and in a teasing manner I said: 'Are you missing your mummy? I will soon be back home.' Little was I to know that they were keeping very bad news from me. My brother-in-law had died two days before and they knew we could not get home for his funeral, as there was only a fortnightly flight from Tenerife in December and, understandably, they did not want to spoil our first exotic holiday. George would have willingly stayed out there for six months in the year, because the climate was kind to his chest complaints. Though it was hot, there was always a lovely breeze from the north African coast, and for many years, he saw himself barefoot again. All those senoritas seemed partial to the Scotsmen.

Everything seemed void of time, but I was really yearning for the green grass of home, and welcomed the snow underfoot when we touched down at Edinburgh airport. I was well versed in the procedures by this time; the best places for exchanging money etc. We looked forward to going back for the sunshine, but it did not live up to my expectations.

It was all so much of a sameness, the same potted plants everywhere always crying out for water. Certainly there were fields of bananas but they did not look any more inviting than a field of turnips at home, as they were all green, and were shipped to our country in that condition. The oranges on the trees were not any more exciting than our own orchards in the autumn.

I felt sorry for the hotel staff who worked extremely hard for very little money and no doubt they resented all the visitors who, to them, had so much money. There was also the language barrier which restricted the conversation. But we did try to convey our appreciation of their services, and we always smiled and gave them many gracious thank yous.

I kept hoping to meet the drunken Scotsmen on the return flight, but goodness knows where they got to.

The journey back was uneventful. We were now seasoned travellers and took advantage of the duty free goods: the scents, watches, drinks and Tenerife whisky at £1.50 a bottle, compared to the £4.50 we had to pay at home.

On our arrival, all the pleasure was knocked off our faces when we realised we had not been there to comfort and support my sister in her loss. A very awkward telephone call followed. No matter how willing one is to hang on to pleasure, or sorrow, other events take over which dim the feelings of both, and that is the pattern of life, nothing stays still.

The arrival of Sybil's youngest, Donna-Louise, helped strengthen the female line of grandchildren, so there was the excitement of a new baby, another girl for Sybil and Hamish, no doubt they were looking for a boy to balance up their own family. There never seemed to be any arguments about the names of the babies as they appeared, compared to what I had to put up with. I did not dictate as to what they should call their children, I would just say, 'Well what are you going to call this one?'

I had now caught the travel bug, and was trying to think of my next jaunt. When George heard it was London he did not fancy it very much. 'Not much sunshine there and no senoritas,' he said. So I went on my own to my sister's, and did a lot of sightseeing. I loved the big antique shops and could hardly believe it when I saw the equivalent of an old chest of drawers I had out in the shed at home. It was quoted at such a ridiculous price. I wish I could have taken mine down as part of my luggage. If I had got the same price it would have meant another holiday to the Grand Canary. I visited Kew Gardens, but what I enjoyed most was the visit to Windsor Castle and its grounds. I by-passed Buckingham Palace as it seemed quite ordinary. Windsor Castle itself is splendid. You could easily imagine all the carriages of yesteryear coming up those beautiful driveways. With nobody in residence it did look cold, as the carpets were all rolled back and the floor boards were bare. So many thousands of feet trampling through, it would have soon worn the carpet to shreds. I was intrigued by the doll's house, which I understood was Queen Mary's. Everything was in that house. What nimble fingers those craftsmen must have had. How many years did those Italian sculptors lie on their backs to decorate those ceilings? There was the Waterloo Chamber, where I believe they used to dine on the anniversary of the Battle of Waterloo. There was also the Tapestry Chamber, the Library, the State rooms, the Red Drawing Room, the Green Room, and the White Drawing Room. I wonder what form of heating was used in those bedrooms in more modern times? It must use so much electricity, as they all look so cold. If my memory serves me correctly, it was used a lot by King George V and Queen Mary. From all accounts it seemed it was their venue for Ascot week when the grounds and gardens would have been at their best and loveliest. I saw it in July. I had a special interest in the chapel, as a local man was the Bishop of Windsor for a time.

One day in Windsor Castle meant more to me than the whole of Tenerife!

In Kew Gardens you could imagine you were visiting each continent of the world, because the vegetables and foliage depicted them for you. And the heat, George would have loved that. I was sad to learn of all the trees uprooted in the hurricanes recently.

I also wanted to see Henley-on-Thames where the regatta takes place. That was fascinating, with all the river house-boats. I do not think I would like to live on one. They looked romantic, away from the madding crowds, but I would prefer to hang out my washing on a clean, green grass. I liked to see all the ducks coming up from the river, they reminded me of my chickens.

Heathrow fascinated me, with the coming and going every minute – and I'm not exaggerating! What a lot of roads there are in the sky, and the brains needed to clear the pathways. But the litter in the streets of London made me relish all the clean roadways at home. I was disappointed in the shops, they just duplicated what was in Edinburgh, Glasgow or Perth, with the exception of hats of course.

To prove what I say is true, I once bought a dress to wear at my Ruby wedding. I saw the duplicate in Perth a week before our celebrations so I went and bought another in a very up market boutique. When my sister came to the Ruby wedding she was more than surprised that I did not wear the dress she had helped me choose in London. I had to explain to her that I was afraid a guest would arrive wearing the same dress. So, good for Scotland I thought, it still provides the goods, and that is one reason why I'm nationalistic.

I have been wined and dined in the poshest of houses but whenever I was ready for my dinner, there was always a lot of chat and wine drinking, which left me desperately hungry as I do not like wine, or should I say, it does not agree with me. So, if I'm ever invited out to dinner, I believe in sitting to eat immediately and doing the drinking afterwards. That, I believe, is the difference between the cuisine of the country yokel, and the city dweller.

Coincidences do happen and that is life. I have seen it many times. Some people call it fate, some people call it religion, but whatever it is there is no denying it happens. For years I had tried hard to keep George's ulcer at bay by careful dieting etc. I've often been annoyed by the physicians' and surgeons' failure to agree on the best way to treat George's problem. However, a day out to Dundee settled the matter. George went to Christine's to while away the time while I was having my hair permed. Whilst there he ate something which made him violently sick and gave him considerable pain. Thanks to Christine's quick action, he was in hospital before my perm was complete. Years of suffering were ended when he was operated on to have his ulcer removed. The operation gave him a new lease of life and gave him greater freedom in what he could eat or drink. Recuperating from the operation was an uphill struggle, especially with the added complication of his chest complaint, but, nonetheless, he was back to work within six weeks. I

51

understand surgery is a risk at any age, but I've often thought that it is a pity fate did not step in much earlier. Following his operation, George made up his mind to make the most of what was left to him and enjoy life as much as he could.

The Welsh grandchildren used to love to see him. It was the highlight of their holiday if 'Hairy Dan' appeared. They had heard all about him from us long before, and had tried to envisage what he looked like. They could not contain themselves when I first introduced him to them. To this day, if he appears in the village, he always enquires about them and their mother. Nomads like him have so much knowledge to impart, if one takes the time to listen to them. Poll tax or income tax will never bother them.

George never took part in sport, he loved to watch it though. Saturday was his heyday, especially if there was football on television. I was a sports widow and no visitors were welcome on a Saturday afternoon, so I usually prolonged my shopping trips, and tried to visit a house where there were no television addicts.

One such typical Saturday I was unable to shop or visit, as I had such an unusual headache that it frightened me, and I was getting on George's nerves with my restlessness. While he was taking down the results for his football coupon, I said: 'I think I'll take a walk down to Shelagh's.'

'I thought you said you had a sore head?' he replied. I did not answer him, and walked out the door as he returned his attention to the results. Shelagh was surprised to see me and asked, 'Is anything wrong?'

'Not really,' I replied. 'But I have a frightening headache on the right side of my head.' Before she could ask if I had taken anything the phone rang. I heard her say to the caller: 'Yes, this is Mrs Robertson speaking,' and then she screamed 'Paula!', threw the phone down, and ran out of the room. I grabbed the phone. I was quite composed, and soon realized I was speaking to Mr Braden, Mhairi's minister. He broke the news to us that Paula had been killed by a car that afternoon.

A bubble burst, for the second time, inside my heart that evening. I have never really stopped crying inside myself, for things never heal in the recess of one's heart. There is a quiet corner of the heart where one's

52

laughter is diminished, forever, because, being a mother, one tries to take on the suffering of others. On reflection, it was extraordinary that that terrible headache, that had disturbed me minutes earlier, completely disappeared as I received that terrible news. How I was given the power and composure to gather Shelagh, George, Grant and Scott, to travel the seventy miles to Broughty Ferry, to meet that terrible grief, I shall never know. The night of the 13th October I will never forget.

My first phone call before we left was to Wales where Colin had to take it as the rest of the family were in London.

Throughout the weeks that followed my eyes were bereft of tears, and it seemed as if I had been given an extra power in the operation of my limbs and mind. Mhairi and Eddie were by this time running a guest house in Broughty Ferry. Despite Paula's tragic death there were still their seventeen lodgers to see to. For the next month this mammoth task was left to George and me.

As I write this, it is the sixth anniversary of Paula's death and each moment I had with her is as vivid today as ever, and her Mum and Dad and brothers are as broken hearted as ever. That teenager, with a Dresden china complexion, would have been a beautiful blonde today, if only she had been spared.

Since that sad day I have had many happy moments but one link of the chain is missing. As I said there is always a sadness in the background. There will be a dimness there forever, especially as someone so young has been taken.

The natural question that people inevitably ask at such a time is, 'Why us, why us?' However, on the other hand, 'Why not us?' Why should people think, or expect, they should be the ones not to have anything to happen to them? One can only share the grief that others suffer, and the whole world admits it is a special grief a mother suffers when a child is taken. All I could do to help was to pray for them. Paula's premature and tragic passing reminded me of a verse:

'Nobody knows what a prayer can do.
When somebody somewhere prays for you.

53

Clearing a path through the tangled track,
Easing the strain on the breaking back.
When hope fades away and is lost to view,
Nobody knows what a prayer can do.'

Mary and George 1939 -
George preparing to go to war.

George, centre back, with his pals in France, 1940.

The Croft in the Hills – Achnahinich, by Plockton

Ann, Sybil and Mhairi 1948.

57

The Croft at Carie – Kinloch Rannoch 1960.

On the farm 1954.

George and Fiona 1968.

The Vagrant 'Hairy Dan'.

'Gitana' – raised after 90 years. December 1983.

L to R: George, Sybil, Mhairi, Ann, Tina, Sheilagh, Mary at grandson David's wedding.

Cutting the Golden Wedding cake.

George and Mary with all the grandchildren at the Golden Wedding.

Lyn on a visit to Kinloch Rannoch

63

Colin going to work in London.

Loch Rannoch with Schiehallion in the background.

64

Chapter 5

Having got back safely from Holland, I sat and reflected on the fun we had had. I had persuaded my friend Nell to go with me at the last minute. With very little time left, she had a rush to get her passport, money changed, and so on and she began to wonder if it was all worth the effort. She also had qualms about flying, and as it had been a last minute arrangement, she did not know who she was to share with. 'Don't worry,' I said, 'I'll arrange it when we get there.'

As we rose in the air, she began to sing, 'Nearer my God to Thee', much to the amusement of all the passengers on the plane. It broke the ice and we were all buddies together by the time we touched down. I spun a story at the hotel reception desk that my friend was very nervous and if it was at all possible, could she share with me? We said we would pay the extra for my supposed partner to take a single room. That would be OK, the receptionist replied. Then we wondered if we would have enough guilders between us to meet that expense. We did hold enough back, but were not asked for them.

The depth of hilarity that developed in that bedroom could not be measured. We saw what looked like an unmade bed, with no top sheet, no blankets, and a white calico-covered quilt folded back. We could not wait to sneak in to other members' rooms to see theirs, all done in the same pattern. There is always a 'know-all' amongst a crowd. She duly enlightened us that they were duvets and we would not require blankets or a top sheet. Being the month of May, it was not that warm, and two people can't parcel themselves in a double duvet, so there was much laughing and fighting for the quilt. Hysterics ensued, as we were now filled with Geneva gin – the cheapest plonk we could afford. Nell's paper money did not last long, her five guilder note she must have thought was five pounds. Being used to bar work at home, she landed behind the hotel bar to help and we all got good measures before the night was out, and it being Scottish custom we each said, 'Have one on us'. I can still feel the belly-ache I had from laughter and the salt tears running into my mouth. I am sure the rest of the hotel guests must have thought, 'Is this how forty Scots women act when together at home?' However, they all appeared to enjoy our singing and dancing.

We toured a diamond factory and I was allowed to be photographed with a most expensive diamond ring on my finger. I felt like Elizabeth Taylor, for a few seconds at least. I also recalled George measuring my finger with a piece of string when he went to buy my engagement ring.

On the day tour to Amsterdam we could not move in the streets, as there were literally thousands of bicycles – from toddlers to grannies. So we had to alter our directions and go down other streets. This proved hilarious to some of the party, who were lured into shops, (practically pulled off the street in fact!) thinking they were cafés, only to discover they were sex aids shops! Nell and I missed out on that, or we might have come home with some more funny stories.

More hilarity as we packed our cases. As I packed mine with extra liquor, such as Advocat and Tia Maria, I thought to myself that if I had the misfortune to be caught I would plead ignorant and say I did not realize they were alcoholic drinks. Everybody hoped I would get caught, but luckily I was not, so I had plenty for a good coffee morning laced with duty free. There was one member who did not want any duty free, so she obliged me by getting extra. Needless to say it was a very jolly coffee morning we organised shortly after we got home.

So to the organisation of the WRI. I gave thanks to those arranged outings and looked to many more. We had risen in the world from our first WRI outing to Blackpool, where four of us ran out of money and had to pawn and sell some of our goods to help us out. Yet the whole weekend only cost us £12. My friend Nell was again the star of the show, but at that time had more control of her money, but not of her laughter – the best tonic in the world.

Is it not good that having reached my three score years and ten, I can look back on those happy times? But, alas, my old pal Nell has now gone.

No more marriages now, so what were to be the next celebrations? There was nothing much in the offing, until we were asked to come down to Colin's eighteenth birthday celebrations. Oh, that long journey to Wales by train – one could fly to the continent quicker! If one lives out on a limb, geographically, one must expect not to travel as the crow flies, so a 7.30 a.m. start ended at 11 p.m.

However it was worth it to see all the youngsters, how they could enjoy themselves! All Colin's pals came to celebrate and partake of food and drinks, produced by Rhae and their good friend Eddie who was chief chef on the barbecue. I was reduced to washer up. The weather was kind to them, and they all ate and drank till they were exhausted. Colin ended up with two birthday cakes, one in the Liverpool FC colours, and another neutral one for those who wanted to partake but were not Liverpool supporters. What good stories cameras tell, they never lie.

It was August so we saw quite a lot of West Wales, Ann being the driver. To me parts of Wales were a miniature Scotland, their language and culture very much different however. Brought up at Loch Carron which was really a sea loch, I was spell bound by the mass of the Irish Sea. I was amused to see the county council road men leaning on such very long-handled shovels. Were they too lazy to bend, or were they more sensible than us, and saved themselves from backache?

My sister was now becoming lonely down south and enjoyed her visits to us. On one of her visits I said to her, 'Why not move up to Scotland?' It took a couple of years to persuade her before she actually took the plunge and bought a house in Broughty Ferry. She was a strong and healthy person, not all aches and pains and digestive problems like me. It was nice to be within travelling distance of one another, as our other sister and brother were living in the USA and Canada. I set her on the path to do bed and breakfasts to pass the time. She had a lovely garden and she was a great gardener. She also enjoyed her short visits to us in this mad house, where there was much hilarity as we had a lot of callers. She always maintained she saw more people in a week in Kinloch Rannoch than she did in a year in Maidenhead. Although she admitted that she enjoyed those visits, she said she would not like to live in the hills.

Shortly after one of her visits, I got a phone call to come down as things were not very good. I could not imagine what had gone wrong in the forty-eight hours since I had seen her. We set off immediately. I do not need to go into detail as to why a certain symptom made her curious enough to consult a doctor, but, in short, this seemingly healthy-looking person was the victim of that dreaded disease, cancer.

How can you tell somebody of seventy years of age, who had never been seriously ill or in hospital, to keep smiling and sweep it under the carpet? The only consolation was that it was caught early.

We gave her all the support we could during her treatment, and took her to her home every weekend. In no time at all she was back in her stride and back to her bed and breakfasts.

I now began to involve myself in politics more and more. I was not a Liberal like my father, or my cousin Alistair MacKenzie, who was Liberal MP for Ross and Cromarty in the 1950s. I did a lot of canvassing for the Scottish National Party, being the secretary or contact for the village. This being a very safe Conservative constituency for many years, we had a real battle on our hands, but with a Liberal and a Labour candidate standing, why not one for the SNP, I thought? When there was a recount, with the SNP and the Tory candidate running neck and neck at the 1983 general election, there was great excitement. However, despite our candidate losing the recount, the gap was certainly closing.

I was more involved than ever in the WRI, being re-elected as President once again. There was also the opportunity of another continental outing. After several suggestions we plumped for Sweden.

We went by coach from Perth to Aberdeen. A very early start, and for me nearly no start at all. I had been laid low with back ache, and had only recovered enough to be able to stand upright two days before we were due to leave for Sweden. With the aid of a stick and some pain killers, I was off on my travels once more!

It looked really misty on the bus journey to Aberdeen. When we arrived we got rid of our luggage and went into the departure lounge. We sat, and we sat, and eventually it was announced that we were to be treated to lunch at the expense of the travel agency, for to our immense disgruntlement, we found ourselves fog-bound. A message was relayed to us to make for the railway station. There was a coach laid on to take us there and our luggage was taken separately in vans. We followed these instructions, only to find our luggage dumped, unceremoniously, outside the station. This was a particularly horrific sight to me, nursing my back ache as I was at the time. How I managed to walk from the entrance to the platform with those cases I do not know. The train we were due to board was for Glasgow. It became apparent that the travel agency had contacted Glasgow airport to charter a plane that was returning with oil workers from Norway. There were only a few seats available on the train, but I managed to secure one. An oil worker became my valet for the journey, carrying my luggage. It was good to pretend that I had a toy boy for the day, and me at fifty-five years of age!

By the time we reached Stravanger in Norway, we were literally starving and there was to be a further two hour coach journey to our hotel in Dals Ed in Sweden. I hastily swallowed a bar of chocolate to keep me going, and another two pain killers. I was the only one who did not feel that journey, and, in fact, felt quite bright as we arrived at our hotel at two o'clock in the morning.

One could travel the world over but you would never get a warmer welcome than we did at that hotel at that hour in the morning. Smiling blonde waitresses waited upon us, and took us into a spacious dining room where our dinner awaited, yes dinner, not breakfast! The hotel was owned by the agency and there must have been a lot of understanding over the telephone from the time we left Aberdeen. No soup or crusty bread ever tasted so good again!

Sweden was entirely different from the Spanish countries I had visited. There was lush green grass and the thousands of little lakes that serviced the main national diet of fish. Smiling blonde waitresses wore blouses and aprons that were whiter than white.

I noticed the absence of litter in the country, I take it people must be fined if they drop any. After covering most of Sweden by coach daily, we went to Norway and sailed up a fjord, which was really splendid. The weather was so perfect everything would have looked good anyway.

We stayed in a hotel called 'Carl XII', which began life as a private house. It was situated between two lakes, Lake Lee and Lake Lilla. During the spring of 1982 there began a new era in the history of this prominent building, when it reopened after complete modernization, offering a successful blend of old tradition with modern comfort. No matter which room you were in, you could look out and see a lake.

It was so nice to recognise some of the old faces amongst the WRI members of Perth and Kinross. We all decided not to talk shop, so rural affairs were left at home. There were the more affluent amongst us, such as the retired school mistress, who possibly had more to spend than the rest of us. Possibly, they had acquired all they ever wanted years ago. I was glad to buy a good watch at duty free prices. Their wants were more in the line of sampling the different wines available, and buying some of the beautiful lace.

Upon my return home, I turned my thoughts as to how I would fund my next continental outing. The first time-share holiday lodges in Britain were built in our village. They offered the locals, especially senior citizens, plenty of work in the way of cleaning and such like. I jumped at the chance to make a few extra pennies. We all thought ourselves as posh 'Mrs Mops' cleaning those luxury residences.

In fact there was little mopping to do as they were all carpeted. Just imagine attacking a chocolate coloured pile carpet to remove the hairs of two moulting cream-coloured labradors, with a machine that made a noise like a helicopter, but which refused to pick anything up? You would wish that it was all mopping! These were just some of the frustrations that met us, but at £1.50 an hour, I had Germany in my sights!

It is a natural instinct of the human being to pretend to the world that things in life are better than they really are, for, of course, that is a question of pride. I was not immune from this dilemma for I began to worry about being able to work, my bad back continued to trouble me, and George's chest complaint became more troublesome. I soon began to think of the things I still wanted to do, and worried about whether I would be able to do them if I was unable to work. I knew I would not be bored. I loved reading and would liked to have had the time to write my memoirs. I was storing all this material in my head, but unfortunately, until now, I never had the time to write. I did have the consolation of my letter writing hobby. George used to say I spent more on stamps than he did on cigarettes. My back trouble came and went, as did George's chest complaint, and thank goodness, I was able to go on working.

I always accepted my life from day to day, and each day was precious to me. I was sometimes uneasy if things ran too smoothly over a long period, because I was always aware of other people's sufferings, and behind everything else, was the knowledge of the deterioration in the condition of our Welsh grandchildren.

Then the inevitable happened. I got word my sister was ill again. Various diagnoses were made but the mention of hepatitis did not sound very good to me. Medical attention, plus our own, could not do much for her. But I must not enlarge on the fate of someone who had reached our allotted life-span, and who had had a comparatively healthy life, plus a two year bonus, following her first illness. I think she was more than glad to be laid to rest beside her husband whom she missed so much, in Kilspindie churchyard at Errol.

After nursing her for a month in her own home in Broughty Ferry, I picked up the threads of my life where I had left off – working and socialising. Every day was now more precious to me than ever. There was the realization that George was also on borrowed time, as the older generation called it. We threw caution to the wind and went to Loret in Spain for the month of February, escaping the worst winter we've had for years.

There seemed to be always a crisis whenever I travelled, and this trip was no exception. The train drivers went on strike for two days, at the very time we were to travel to Gatwick. After some desperate phone

71

calls, SAGA managed to get us seats on a bus from Aberdeen. There were only two bus services operating at the time and we blessed them.

Shelagh took us to Perth to meet the coach at 9.05 p.m. It was a very nasty night with rain and sleet and on the way, to our horror, we had a puncture. The boot was loaded with our cases and we had no torch. George was determined to turn back. Shelagh ran a quarter of a mile, through sleet and rain, to a farmhouse, where she was able to get help to change the tyre. We eventually got to Perth with three minutes to spare!

We arrived in London at 7 a.m. where the bus parked on some waste ground (the bus service did not even have a depot at this time!) We made our way to the underground station, laden with luggage, to catch a train to Gatwick. We thought we would be made into mincemeat on that train, with the early morning rush of commuters. We were just about ready to collapse. People were jumping in and out like frogs. We did not even know which stop to come off at, until eventually an elderly coloured man came to our rescue and indicated the stop we needed. I could have kissed him with gratitude! If we had come on the train to London, a SAGA representative would have met us, and taken us on a coach to Gatwick. It would have been all so much more civilized.

A month in the sunshine of Loret made us forget all the harassment we had suffered and we were able to rest easy in the knowledge that there would not be a similar problem on our journey home – or so we hoped!

George slipped and hurt his back while we were in Loret, so he had to buy a walking stick and was not much use for handling luggage, and so on.

We were lucky we did not become flu victims while we were there, as many English visitors came across with flu. Many were very ill and some even died. We were much relieved to be fit to come home.

It was a beautiful, crisp day when we arrived back in London on 2nd March. You may think this is a joke, but believe it or not, we had arrived home to a one-day London bus strike, of all things! So instead of five buses waiting for SAGA members, there was one, and that was for the use of the oldest members only. George's stick and slow gait served us well, and thankfully, we were able to get a seat on that bus. We left

72

absolute chaos behind.

I never imagined that there were so many taxis in all the world as I saw in London that day. It took hours for the bus to get into city, because we could not move for the sheer number of taxis around. They were like a mass of black beetles. All I could do was sit and laugh.

The driver of the bus said to me, 'Where are you going to, love?' 'To Scotland,' I replied. 'I hope the trains are OK again.' He did not know.

We missed our earlier train and had to wait until 11 p.m. which meant spending hours at Euston station. This was a terrifying experience. George was in a lot of discomfort with his injured back, which meant he had to spend a lot of time in the café. We were not able to stay at one table for long, and had to keep moving on to another. It was a merry-go-round of endless cups of tea. There were so many drop-outs and weird people in and out of the café, grabbing the crusts we left behind, and drinking the dregs we left in our cups. The police moved them on, only for them to be replaced by many more, asking for cigarettes and money. We took refuge in a lounge bar, but we nearly choked at the price of half a pint, and still the weirdos appeared and molested us.

George kept muttering that if ever he got back in one piece, he would never ask to leave home again. I could not keep myself from laughing, and he replied that he felt very much like crying. I was so glad to leave London, but at the same time, glad I witnessed what I did. It was terrible to see human beings reduced to grovelling for food in this day and age. It may have been the case that it was their own fault they were in such circumstances, I don't know. They seemed clean enough to me.

We were glad to get on that train and have a carriage to ourselves. We were exhausted and ready for a sleep, and looked forward to a cup of tea in the morning. We were in for a double shock. At about six o'clock we wakened with an awareness that the train had stopped. Soon afterwards the guard came into every carriage to inform us that the points were frozen and we could not move till somebody came on duty at such and such a time. I said, 'You're joking!' 'No my dear, I am not,' he replied. We asked him when the buffet would be open only to discover, to our horror, that there was not one on the train. Imagine, a train from London to Inverness, in the month of March with no buffet carriage! I said to the guard, 'Do you realise we left Loret yesterday morning, and we're still travelling!' He offered us a cup of tea out of his own flask, but we declined. I was so thirsty, but could not bring myself to drink the water on the train. Thank goodness for our Spanish oranges, and duty free brandy. We were still stuck on the train at Lockerbie at 8 a.m. when we should have been at Pitlochry where Shelagh was waiting for us, unaware of our delay.

We did not arrive home till noon and we returned to a waterless house. Our water pipes had been frozen for six weeks. We did look funny with our tanned faces amongst the frozen snow and ice. One day we were on holiday in the lap of luxury, and the next, carting water from the river to wash and drink with. They say variety is the spice of life!

George had by now given up his hotel work so he had to amuse himself somehow with domestic chores at home. Thus, there was little for me to do now when I returned home from work. There was still a trickle of bed and breakfasts throughout the season which helped to boost my morale, and my purse.

There was always a great number of friends visiting us. The visitors we used to have on the croft were now sending their offspring to call on us. I was supposed to remember their faces after thirty years, them being only children when I saw them last.

Even the vagrant 'Hairy Dan', who had helped us on the croft, gave us a yearly call when was on his rounds. When he called I would ask him to hack some sticks, or muck out the byre, in return for some tea and something to eat. One day, after mucking out the byre, I offered him a bar of soap and a towel, to go and wash himself in the burn before eating. 'Oh no missus,' he said. 'A wash would be the death of me!' On reflection, when I recall what I could see of his face and hands, his skin appeared petal soft. Though born in a tent, he had fought in the war, and he played the bagpipes. His constant companion was his dog, and if he did not like some of his sandwiches, he would give them to him. His proper name was John MacDonald, and I think this gave him an affinity with us.

One dare not be too confident about anything. Our Ruby wedding was on the horizon and we sat and reflected on what we had been through and how much we had to be thankful for. Since George's operation we had the joy of seeing Shelagh married, but gey loath we were to part with our baby. We secretly hoped we could have had her for just a few more years.

First anniversaries are usually a highlight but Shelagh made it a double highlight by producing her first born, Grant. Yes, yet another boy. The granddaughters were having an uphill struggle to compete, there was no catching up on all those little boys now.

Shelagh had completed her hairdressing training and she did not want to let it go for long. So, while we were planning our Ruby celebrations in advance, she had another race on, to complete her family before she went back to work. Her second son Scott was born in October.

Here we were, about to celebrate forty years of marriage, and were grandparents to fifteen grandchildren. I was determined to buy a gown to 'de-granny' myself, and that is exactly what I did. I spent more on it than I will ever do again and yet it has had only one airing.

Ruby weddings are much the same as ordinary weddings, a meeting of the family plus a few special friends. The younger generation were not there, except for Lyn. However, I said to myself, 'Never mind, they will be all old enough to attend our Golden wedding if spared and well.' And that is what happened, except for the fact that one link of the chain was missing, which I will come to later.

Where are all my diaries of those years? Either they were lost in our house moves, or they ended up as scribbling pads for the children. I was talking recently to a psychologist who told me that a person learns more between the age of six months and six years than in the rest of their lives. I said, 'But what about the memory bank, why do I remember childhood incidents, but not something that happened ten years ago?' 'Well,' he says, 'If you live to be a hundred and twenty, you will possibly remember things you knew at seventy.' That I will never know, because I will not live to that age and will not be able to prove his point.

The Ruby wedding was special, in the sense that the Minister who married us was able to be with us once again, being quite a young man when he performed the first ceremony. We also had our bridesmaid with us to celebrate, but unfortunately our best man was unable to come because of ill health. Sybil was also ill and unable to make the journey from her home in Edinburgh. I did not seem to lose the mantle of mother and kept a watchful eye on everybody at the celebrations to ensure they did not blot their copy books. However, my watchful gaze did not go far enough to keep tabs on George, who nearly required resuscitating during the night after almost swallowing his false teeth. We all stayed in the hotel overnight and I think I was the only one who enjoyed my breakfast. Let that statement speak for itself!

Weddings usually have honeymoons, and Ruby weddings were no exception. George and I set off for Spain. By now we were more experienced fliers, and familiar with the travel procedures and the foreign food. We made sure we had our own tea bags and Marvel milk. We would buy water and make our own tea in our hotel room. It was nice, I thought, to get away after all the excitement of the previous six weeks – Scott's arrival and the Ruby wedding celebrations.

On entering our hotel room we thought we had the wrong key. There was a bottle of champagne on a silver tray, with two champagne glasses and a card. 'Oh!' I said. 'We are in the wrong room.' Then we spotted the name of MacDonald on the envelope, I took out the card and it read, 'Lots of love from the girls', signed by them all individually. They had obviously made good use of the information about the hotel we naturally gave them before we left. 'Too bad if this goes on my bill,' I said, but it did not. The management made sure we had a lovely evening, and we certainly did. They announced that it was our Ruby wedding to several other British guests, and plied us all with wine. I said earlier on I do not like wine, or rather it does not like me, but I did not want to appear choosy so I did partake, and, believe me, nobody has ever had such a headache as I had the following morning! We certainly lost a day's sunshine, the only consolation being that I was not alone in suffering with the effects of a hangover. I took home the two champagne glasses, only to discover in our gifts, that we had already had a set. However, none of them have been christened with champagne, as that first taste did not appeal to me and I made a point of never buying it again – not even for the glasses I now own.

On our return I opened all the gifts, which were very unusual and of such value that I could not possibly hide them away in a drawer out of sight. So I invested in a unit to display them all and threatened anybody to touch them. They were all pleasing to the eye but far too good for daily use.

We were now back to old clothes and porridge. No more babies on the way, so we settled down to the humdrum way of life, as we began to realise we were ageing grandparents.

Boredom soon set in. However, the WRI gave me food for thought when I discovered the group were arranging a trip to Holland. That sounded like the dreams I had of seeing the bulb fields many years earlier. I held back for many weeks before telling George about the trip. When I did, I said, 'The WRI are going on an outing in May, I think I will put my name down, it is only a weekend.' 'Where are they going?' he says. 'Well, I am not sure yet,' I said. 'It is either Edinburgh or Aberdeen.' It was not really a fib as we would be leaving from one airport or the other.

The family only believed that I'd been in Aberdeen for a weekend until I returned and produced the duty free goods and the Delft pottery. Thinking I was in Aberdeen, they could not fathom out the post card I sent them from Holland.

Whilst I was there I discovered that there was not such a thing as the pure black tulip, it is a very dark navy blue. When you are passing the fields on the bus they all look like black tulips, but on closer inspection, they are navy blue. Holland is a very clean country with no litter to be seen anywhere. I don't think there are as many bicycles anywhere in the world as I had seen there – from toddler to granny bicycles. I believe it is because Holland is such a flat country. There was a bicycle demonstration in Amsterdam when we were there. This was a demonstration against all the taxis who often knock cyclists down. I thought it was put on especially for our sake. As we were leaving the airport, we had a good view of Rotterdam, and could hardly believe that it was all built up again after being flattened in the war.

Thanks to the organisation of the WRI group we had a marvellous and well organised tour, at a very modest cost. We were all looking forward to our next outing, providing I was ever allowed to go again! A good courier is a great bonus on such trips. They are able to tell us of the customs of the country and what the equivalent is of our health service, pension schemes, work etc. This gave us a good insight into the Dutch way of life.

Chapter 6

I think I should write down the following if by chance fate should intervene, and I do not get the opportunity later.

At the moment my heart is bursting with pride that Colin, my disabled grandson, has, after a lot of disappointments, managed to get himself a job with Radio Four in London. He is entirely dependent on complete strangers to be his carers. I hope at a later date to write more about that. I will now go back to where I left off, if my memory will allow me.

Shelagh and Gus were now living in Rannoch, having come from Dundee, and their two little boys, Grant and Scott, gave us an added interest.

There was no hairdresser in the village so Shelagh had a good opportunity to start a business. The boys were not yet school age so she had the benefit of us to look after them. This indeed was a morale booster for George in his enforced retirement, caring and attending to two boys after rearing five girls.

He found them so interesting and they found their Grandpa equally interesting, with his quotes and advice, very alien to what they heard from their parents. Lots of it they queried, as for instance, 'Why did Grandpa say such and such?' or 'Grandpa says so and so.'

Scott at four years of age, while looking at his grandfather's hands, which were very lined with enlarged veins said, 'Why do you have so many worms and roads on your hand, Grandpa?'

This quite stunned George, who was not aware the advancing years were so prominent, and after much thought he said, 'People get old, Scott, and their skin becomes lined.' 'Oh,' said Scott. 'Will they soon be taking you up in a helicopter to heaven?' I do not think he was in much favour for a few days.

We were both so grateful that throughout the years, we were always able to see quite a lot of our grandchildren, and now this was the icing on the cake, having the two little boys in the village.

Another bright star on the horizon was that Colin chose Stirling University to come and study in. This meant he could come for a weekend and we could visit him. This was an act of courage for a person so disabled to come 400 miles from his home in West Wales and be dependent on carers.

Stirling University, being built on different levels, was very suitable for a wheelchair, no steps or stairs. The only thing was the dorms were very small and did not give much room for a wheelchair to manoeuvre. But it was adequate for Colin's needs.

Another grandson, Jason, was studying for Hotel Management and did a season in the local hotel. So, there again, we saw another of them grow up, all little bonuses.

It was coming up to the first anniversary of Paula's death, and being relaxed and not busy, I relived that awful day and the weeks following it. Shortly after that I began to feel unwell, not my usual condition, and could not pin it to any of my usual symptoms. I began to think it was delayed reaction, as I seemed to shed the tears I did not shed the year before, and maybe I had not been made of tougher material after all.

I was beginning to accept it was delayed reaction and not depression, so I began to think the answer was simple, I had to get it out of my system and get new interests. I began arranging a Burns' Night for an Open Night at the WRI, and the majority of the committee being English, left it to the old Scottish member to get on with it.

I had to find out how much I was allowed to spend on artists and then revolve everything around that. I picked the best and the most expensive artists who did kindly reduce their usual fee. Everything was going according to plan for the night in January. All the Christmas festivities were looming up, children's parties, dinner dances etc, all of which I was looking forward to, but all my every day chores were becoming a burden to me, and I could not think why.

On the morning of December 12th, I was looking through my wardrobe to see what I was going to wear to the Senior Citizens Dinner Dance that evening, when I collapsed. On coming round, and waiting for the doctor, I put it down to a change of tablets I had taken the night before, and that morning, for my arthritis. The doctor when he arrived said, 'Well, we shall put a red line against those, just rest for this afternoon and you will possibly make it for tonight.' Needless to say I did not and could not use my legs or descend the stairs for two days. I laughed about it, and said to my neighbour, 'Imagine two tablets having that effect.' 'You're possibly allergic to them,' she said.

It took me a week to get going again and yet I did not have the zest for things. Taking down the Christmas decorations was beyond me, I did not seem to have the breath for it, and now it was slowly dawning on me, it could not have been the tablets.

I had promised myself I would seek medical advice, but each day I pushed myself a little further and got on with the arrangements for our Burns' Night, but the Monday before it I collapsed again and this time I knew it was not the tablets.

I was gasping for breath and confined to bed with antibiotics, and ordered to stay put, that's all I could do. After two days, my brain was working overtime for the function, and the committee was very anxious, as they had left everything to me. I knew I could not chair the meeting now, but I was desperately wanting to be fit to attend if nothing else. Friday saw me downstairs, my daughter, my husband and the doctor ordering me to stay put.

The minister called the evening before, and also suggested I should not go. 'Well,' I said, 'you are going, and so is the doctor, so the two most important people will be there if I need help.'

Another 24 hours made me feel slightly better, but I did not have the strength to dress up for it, so I went with the old tartan skirt and jacket. It was a marvellous evening and everything went very well. The artists were outstanding but I did not have the strength to clap or laugh, and bed was never so welcome. Then I realised there was a lot wrong with me by my pallor and lack of strength, so when the doctor called on Monday I told him how I felt. He immediately sent me to Perth Royal Infirmary for tests which revealed I had an enlarged heart and fluid on the lungs, in other words I had heart failure.

It took me weeks to manipulate a duster or go outside the door. This certainly shook my confidence and I began to look at everything in a different light.

I now realised what shortness of breath was, and thought of the years George had suffered with it, but the roles were now reversed, he was my mentor. I have just realized that I started my memoirs with the memory of the 'Clouds of War', and as I write this, there is again the threat of war in the Persian Gulf. We live with the knowledge of the threat every day for months. Was my ignorance of the last war the best? I think so.

I was warned if I slowed down and took things very canny, I would soon lead as normal a life as possible, just a quiet living housewife. I did comply with the rules and felt better for a few weeks, and then stalemate for week upon week and by May month I had to attend Perth Royal Infirmary again, only to discover their medication was now the trouble, administered for too long, until it took all the potassium out of my body.

With that put right I began to climb the ladder again slowly, and gave up all social activities, such as hostessing, history class, WRI President and work that earned some pennies.

I had one ambition left and that was to visit Austria. I knew that was coming up on the horizon with the WRI so I was extremely careful with this in mind.

With a confirmed hiatus hernia I had difficulty in managing a proper diet that would not affect me, as my enlarged heart and hiatus hernia lay side by side, and not much room for both when my hernia was active.

I was not allowed to do much physically but I could use my brain and the task I was given was to arrange a wedding for my grandniece who worked in Turkey, and marrying a Turk. She was a flower girl to my daughter Ann, over twenty years ago. She decided she would like a similar wedding here in Scotland, and especially Rannoch so she phoned to see what I could do about it. I said to leave it to me, all arrangements, catering, accommodation, minister, piper, travel facilities, I took everything on board. Many slips and hiccups along the way, but nothing that could not be resolved in time. People were coming from Germany, Turkey, Wales and London so it really was an international event, one guest even came from New Zealand, and Julia's air hostess sister, Fiona, flew in from Pakistan for the wedding. She had to leave again the next day, bound for Los Angeles.

Battel, the groom, was delighted and so were his Turkish guests, they were absolutely charmed to be attending a typical Scottish wedding.

The local people put them through their paces when it came to dancing, and who do you guess was not able to dance? Days before the wedding I took an excruciating pain in my knee, I thought I had thrombosis, so I called the doctor who said I had fluid on the knee, and was to rest with my leg up on a chair. So poor George again was host to people arriving and having a cup of tea before they went to their booked accommodation.

I hobbled out of the car on the day of the wedding, with a cane for support. I could not even dance a waltz that night, but with everything going so well I really did not mind. I just sat back and enjoyed seeing others enjoying themselves. I organised a video to be taken of the wedding from the service onwards, so that the Turkish people could see it.

I said to myself, this is a wee message to me to take things easy, fluid on the knee! It kept me confined to barracks. I was possibly climbing the ladder too quickly, so I stayed on this rung all summer, feeling very frustrated. I did some knitting and a lot of reading and enjoyed having Colin from his break from Stirling University.

Anyway, I recovered enough to make the trip to Austria. I would not have missed this for anything. The cleanliness and the beauty of the country was outstanding. I thought we had a majestic mountain overlooking Rannoch, but now it looked just like a hill compared with those miles of such mountains, as if they were drawn by pencil and nestled between them were these lonely little valleys, with tiny rivers running along them. Tiny wooden houses and cows grazing among the lush green grass.

In Innsbruck the pavements were broader than the streets in our cities and there again no litter to be seen. I do not think the fact that Margaret Thatcher had been there at the beginning of the week made them so clean. Her visit might have affected the prices which were beyond our purses.

We paid a visit to Italy where we got better value for our money, and we found the people who served in the shops were very helpful – maybe they like the Scottish accent – we also found the same in Germany and Austria, that they liked the Scots people.

I could have done a lot more day trips, but I was frightened to tire myself. We had lots of fun amongst ourselves and it was interesting to meet so many other nationalities in the hotels. The majority of them could speak English, seemingly it is compulsory to take it in school after the age of twelve.

As I mentioned earlier on, it is imperative to have a good courier on these tours, and we again were lucky. We found out a lot of the customs of the country from her. One day we stopped at a small town while she ran into a store and came out with dozens of candles. We asked her what she was going to do with all the candles, she said they were for her aunt who kept candles lit all night in the churchyard, possibly on her husband's grave. Apparently she could not get candles in the district where she lived. They must do a roaring trade in candles in that country if this is the tradition.

I was glad to be home again and though I enjoyed seeing the country, I could not enjoy the evenings and after dinner when the others were preparing for a social gathering, I slipped away to bed, everybody querying as to where Mrs Mac had gone. I did not disclose when I was asked each morning, 'Now where did you disappear to?' 'Oh,' I said. 'That would be telling!' and gave them the impression I was at some other interesting venue.

I found it quite interesting helping some of my friends convert their money, but on the last day they had the last laugh on me. A few of us were in this gift shop, we were all so interested in the delicate hand painted china ornaments etc, mostly done in Germany. We realized they were very expensive. I helped two ladies convert their last lot of spending money, at the same time my eye was on these two delicate painted egg cups and their stands. We all admired them, and I quickly converted the money in my mind, told the gentleman to box them for me while I helped the other two ladies. He did them up beautifully and then quoted X number of schillings. I stood and stared and again asked how many schillings. He repeated the same number and I nearly dropped them. It worked out at £13 sterling, for two egg cups and their tiny stands. If he had not had them wrapped up, I would not have taken them. My friends burst out laughing and said, 'Who understands the currency now? At least we admit we don't.' I was concentrating so much on them, I blundered with myself. Needless to say, the humble egg has never graced them and recently a lady who collects egg cups was looking in my china cabinet, and said, 'Oh, look at those egg cups.' 'Do you like them?' I said. 'Oh, they are really delicate.' 'Well you can have them for your 70th birthday this week, but do not drop them, they are priceless.' My other souvenir of Austria is my Tyrolean hat, complete with feather, and a linen tea cloth and napkins.

I took things very canny and did just what was necessary. I took up knitting, not that I am a good knitter, but I found it relaxing, but soon had to give it up. I had what some people would call a frozen shoulder. So I resorted to reading and television and it was one evening reading a book at bedtime, when suddenly back came that pain at 11 p.m. George quickly phoned the doctor, who was there in five minutes, and after a couple of injections, I felt relief, but had a bad night, so was confined to bed again for a couple of weeks. I felt great disappointment, as I had been leading a quiet life. I did have difficulty with my hiatus hernia and a lot of discomfort, depending on what I ate. I was so sorry to be giving such worry to George who found it difficult to climb the stairs to attend to me. The difficulty also being that the toilet and bathroom were downstairs. Fortunately, I still held on to a commode.

After about ten days I was beginning to recover when one night, at 11 p.m. there was a loud knocking at the front door. I heard it from my bed.

My daughter, Mhairi, had come to see me and stayed the night. She switched on the light and went downstairs, her legs like jelly, reluctantly to open the door. I heard her say: 'Oh, Mam!' and then silence. I nearly did have a heart attack in bed then until I realized what was happening. On hearing I was ill again, Ann, Rhae and Lyn had travelled up from Wales. It shows how bad I felt, I could not even get out of bed to see them, but thankfully Mhairi was there to see to beds. George was not much use either, except to put on the kettle. This made me more frustrated than ever, I could not do anything to help domestically.

From then on, I realized I would have to be a lady of leisure. I was told not to bend, slacken my step etc. All that took a lot of adjustment. Holiday brochures came in, I would browse through them and then they went in the bin. But I still had a secret I was not willing to disclose. Seeing how I managed to go to Austria, I had put my name down for Yugoslavia, for the following May. The WRI always needed the names so far in advance to see if the trip was viable. As the doctor kept a check on me, I said, 'I think in the spring, maybe April or May, I will visit my relative in Canada, do you think that would be advisable?' 'Well, that depends on you,' he said, 'We shall see how you behave between now and then, but I do not see why not.' Anyway, I had broken the ice to him and George that I would probably be on the move again in the spring. If the doctor had said, 'No way' I would have cancelled it at that time.

Having this little secret kept up my spirits throughout the winter and the pennies were secretly put by. I was not going out to spend anyway. I was the only one going from Rannoch WRI, so it did not leak out.

Chapter 7

As I write I feel I may be missing out on detail, but no matter, how much I may be prepared to tell of myself, (and I would prefer to tell all), I do not wish to involve others. I prefer to present an overall picture. I feel it to be inappropriate, and maybe an act of discourtesy, to write of living persons in a memoir of this kind. Since I cannot tell all I believe it is best to say nothing, other than family details. So this is not going to be a best seller, besides, there are not enough juicy bits in it!

I was now reconciled to an increasingly inactive life, physically I mean. But my mind was as alert as ever. It was at this point that I began to sense that there was something I had not yet achieved, that something was missing, that I may have been ready to leave this world before realising what it was.

Thank goodness for reading material. That winter I realised I must slow down; I was neither a knitter nor a sewer; I did not bake now, for if I baked I ate, and I was fighting the battle of the bulge, so I passed the time reading and writing letters. I got myself a typewriter, and had lots of fun with it. The letter 'p' more often became a 'q' and the letter 'g' became a 'h'.

My friends and family did not like my typewritten letters. They felt them cold and the news they contained wasn't homely. To some people letters, like food, must be pleasing to the eye to be enjoyable.

It was the beginning of another year, what would it bring along? January is usually a very cold month and January 12th 1987 was the coldest day in Britain for fifty years. We had a three hour power cut. It did not bother us much until we realised that we would not have electric blankets that night. We quickly looked out the hot water bottle and very clumsily tried to boil a pan of water on the fire for our supper. The water tasted a bit smoky in the tea, but it was at least hot, and we were most grateful for it. I prepared another pan to fill the flask for the morning, but hurrah! – the power came back on again. I sat back and reflected on how I managed without electricity all those years ago. I then realised I had a proper cooking range or rayburn cooker, not a small lounge fire to balance a pan on. I guess any house with a coal fire is a bonus.

The following day the coalman brought us a surprise – an extra two bags of coal – a gift from the Francis Gay Fund. Why me? I said. The coalman explained that he put all his customers' names forward and picked a number out. This time I was one of the lucky ones. I sent him a letter of thanks via the *Sunday Post*.

The winter was long and driech and was compounded by the fact that my friend Nell was feeling below par. However, we had each other's company, and reminisced a lot – at times in tears, others at heights of hilarity, and sometimes in utter despair for Nell. I tried very hard to raise her spirits and often as not succeeded in doing so.

I was glad of the company of my two youngest grandsons in the afternoons when they came home from school. They liked to hear stories of my childhood and their questions were many and varied. I am sure they did not believe half of my replies from the smirks that came on their faces and their long ponderous silences. They certainly did not believe me when they asked how much pocket money I got at their age. I said I did not get any. 'Surely you got something Granny?' they said. 'No, I did not,' I replied. 'I possibly got a new pair of shoes when a calf was sold, and that was excitement enough to a girl always wearing tackety boots.' I continued: 'We got a penny or two half pennies because sometimes I could keep one back if I was smart enough.' This caused a lot of giggles and furrowed brows. Then they would quiz me a bit further, and say, 'What about holidays, surely you got something for that?' 'I did not go on holidays,' I replied. There followed more guffaws and long silences where you could almost read their thoughts – You must be kidding Granny!

Another Grandson, David, appeared on the horizon. At eighteen years of age he decided to come and work in a hotel in Rannoch. How would he like to be within his Granny's clutches I wondered? By his daily visits it didn't seem to bother him. He agreed with everything I said or suggested – possibly the easiest way to keep my favour!

There followed a particularly cold spell that kept George indoors for many weeks. However, we had so many callers coming in and out with their coughs and sneezes that George was inevitably infected, the result being yet another chest infection. He was so prone to infection I think I would really require a guard on the door to permit entry only to people with infection free passports!

Colin and his helper arrived from Stirling University for David's eighteenth birthday party. This cheered George a lot, but he was not going to be fit to go out to the party, which put a slight dampener on the occasion for all concerned.

A few days later I happened to be going out to the shop. Two doors away, as the youngsters were going out for a walk, I spotted a car drawing up and a lady got out and went into the shop. I recognised the driver of the car immediately – it was the singer Andy Stewart whom George admired greatly. I immediately took the bull by the horns and approached the driver, 'Andy, excuse me for invading your privacy, but would you do me a great favour? My husband is a great fan of yours and he has been quite ill and could do with a boost. I think a quick visit from you would do as much good as any medicine.' 'Certainly,' Andy replied. 'What's his name?'

As I opened the living room door, and ushered the visitor in, I said, 'Here is someone to see you, George.' There was no response as he sat glumly and blankly looking at the visitor. Gradually, a glimmer of recognition began to creep across his face. I cannot describe the state of shock followed by ecstasy that erupted in that living room that afternoon. Andy stayed a few minutes chatting to George before making his apologies that he was unable to stay any longer. However, to put the icing on the cake, he returned a couple of minutes later with his teenage daughter, complete with instamatic camera. She took a photo of Andy and George together. As he left I thanked him profusely, and said his visit had done more good for George than any doctor's treatment. 'Och well,' Andy replied, 'you have a very good doctor up here, he attended me when I was on holiday last year.'

Needless to say Andy and George were no Clark Gables in the photo. Andy had aged much with his grey hair, and three weeks of coughing for George did nothing for his appearance.

When the boys returned from their walk we had a story to tell them. I piped up as they entered, 'We had a visitor when you were out.' 'That's not unusual in this house,' Colin replied. 'Who was it this time?' 'Andy Stewart,' I told him. 'Oh Granny stop havering, we have only been away half an hour, and Grandpa was asleep when we left.' 'A lot can happen in ten minutes, far less half an hour,' I told him. 'Well, whoever it was, Grandpa certainly looks better,' Colin observed. When I completed the story of Andy's visit Colin said: 'Oh Granny, it's only you that would pull stars off the street!'

Those little incidents helped to brighten our lives.

It was soon spring again and the crocuses and tulips were there once again to wash away all our usual aches and pains that gathered during the winter. With my secret trip to Yugoslavia approaching my spirits rose, but I didn't want to show too much enthusiasm after all my grumbles throughout the winter. I packed my case very stealthily, as if I was packing the Crown Jewels, and then calmly announced that I would be off to Yugoslavia the following week. George looked up from his paper and said, 'Oh you are going are you, are you fit?' 'Well, I will be going, I'll just not do any sightseeing that's all,' I retorted. With the ice broken I was more active in my preparation. I went to the bank to exchange some money. The thought of the journey to Glasgow airport one hundred miles away was daunting, but forty cackling women soon make you forget any misgivings.

The flight was good and uneventful. The hotel was first class. There were no late sessions and sing songs for me on this trip, nor did I put my name down for day trips or folk dancing. When I disappeared from the company they thought I had some secret rendezvous. I used to be the life and soul of the party on former trips and they simply couldn't understand why I kept disappearing so early each evening.

As usual I was interested in observing the culture of the country. How hard they worked for so little money. Personal items were more important to the hotel staff than money. We usually gave them what was left of their currency, but our courier advised us that personal items were of more value. So, the tights, talc and soap I had not used were all left behind, and no doubt gratefully received.

Yugoslavia was yet another country I had discovered that really welcomed Scottish visitors. In shops and restaurants we were asked: 'Are you English?' 'No, Scottish,' we replied. This immediately marked us out for special service for some peculiar reason. Did they think we parted with our money more easily? If so, they obviously hadn't heard the one about the mean Scot!

I was glad to get home safely, and fully realized that this must be the end of my gallivanting. A birthday too many maybe.

Chapter 8

It saddens me to hear children in this affluent society saying they are bored. We never had time to feel bored because we made our own entertainment and enjoyed it.

Today there are too many bought toys and too much canned entertainment, so that no child has the challenge to create their own. I compare what my children did to amuse themselves, and what their children do at present.

The access to television certainly helps to stimulate their brains in many ways and they possibly can converse with their elders on many subjects they might not have known about, but for television.

It's the lack of exercise that worries me, as they seem to spend so many hours watching television, instead of out playing games. My own grandchildren locally are boys, and they do play a lot of football which is good exercise.

My big question now was what would I do for exercise now that I was more or less grounded from doing many tasks. The simplest and cheapest method was walking, a good pair of brogues, a light stick and I was off. It was pleasant on a nice day, but who likes walking in the rain? I don't.

Referring back to television, it also has its influence on me. Many years ago going to church was great relaxation for me for an hour, and to come home and just sit down to dinner, having timed the potatoes for my arrival, (you can guess I cooked the dinner before I left). This was more for a rest than spiritual healing, if I picked some up, good and well.

As the years rolled by I still liked going, not to get away from children, but for many other reasons: to be in harmony with the rest of the people; to find encouragement and examples in my daily needs, some examples coming from the pulpit I hoped! You can gather from my story I flitted a lot and so listened to many ministers.

Now with television and radio I can get all from both if I so wish and it's nice to sit and relax after a bath in my dressing gown, and get spiritually fed and sit quietly and think deeply of what I had just heard. William Barclay had a great influence on me and explained the Bible so well. Then often my conscience pricks me and the next Sunday I go to church with the television sermon very much uppermost in my mind and ready to compare it with what I am about to hear.

Does it mean people are taken over by television on a Sunday morning, and is this the cause of the falling church membership? Is it that the church has lost its reverence with the number of women elders? Being a mere woman I should not comment on it, but I do. I myself do not approve of them. They do fill the necessary role behind the scenes but despite the fact there are many women elders in a large proportion of the church today, this has not halted the decline in membership. So, where are the men?

Still on the theme of television, 1987 was quite an exciting year with another election to take place. As citizens of today we have the opportunity our forefathers did not have. How they would have loved to have seen Lloyd George or Winston Churchill being interviewed. As an SNP supporter, I quite enjoyed seeing Margaret Thatcher and Neil Kinnock being interviewed, and did not bother how much they were harassed by the interviewer. I did take note of how clever each was in evading the majority of questions asked. I used to think Harold Wilson was very clever at that, but Thatcher and Kinnock were equally clever, each having their own way of doing so, Margaret more on attack than Kinnock.

However, something much more important than an election was looming on the horizon – our Golden Wedding. Healthwise, I had had so many ups and downs, all I wished was to be able to live to celebrate it quietly with George. The weather was cold and in my plans if spared and well in the spring, there would be a get together of all friends and relations, as the days lengthened again. It's good to be spared and well to reach that goal anyway.

It so happened that any celebrations were put very much out of my mind as we were worried about Colin. He was at Stirling University and not well and was admitted to the Infirmary, his parents having to come up from Wales to see him. His other brother, Alan, had just fallen and broken his ankle causing their parents a terrible dilemma, torn both ways with five hundred miles to cover. This did not help my condition and I decided I must be the centre of attraction by taking another slight turn that made Shelagh seek the doctor – this being ten days before I might have celebrated my Golden Wedding by having a quiet family dinner. The usual advice was given – stay quiet, no talking, and no visitors. This I was glad to adhere to as I could not do anything else.

The end of November brought some early Christmas cards, especially from abroad. Some cards arrived which I couldn't be bothered to look at, and when I did, realized they were Congratulation cards for fifty years of marriage, and from people about whom I began to wonder, 'How could they remember we were fifty years wed?'

I sat and planned what form of celebration we would have in the spring of the following year, so that young and old could enjoy themselves. What would I wear, and where would the celebrations be, so that it would be convenient to all who would have to travel a distance?

This gave me food for thought and dispelled all the worries I might have had to celebrate at the appropriate date.

Then, out of the blue, comes a letter from Ann in Wales, saying, 'We will be up on Saturday to have dinner with you and do not bother about accommodation.' I was panic stricken, the thought of food itself made me ill, as I could not think of swallowing anything other than the meagre diet I arranged for myself. I was really annoyed and showed the letter to the doctor, and said, 'Look at that, and you tell me to stay quiet and not a lot of talking.' I was possibly annoyed that it was upsetting my plans, and pleasant as it would be for family all to come, I very much wanted old friends and neighbours. I sat very sullen all week, and did not take much notice of all the cards coming in.

94

Our family from Wales arrived on the Friday night and had obviously booked into the Dunalistair Hotel where no doubt we were to have our meal on the Saturday.

I was more or less confined to barracks on the Saturday, not allowed out, this was their way of protecting me I thought as I went to go for a spool for the camera. 'No, no, so and so is going across anyway, they will get it.' At this point I thought they were over-protective, and when I realised all family and all grandchildren were coming, this again filled me with sadness because the missing link in the chain, Paula, was not there. How would Mhairi and Eddie bear up?

I saw them arrive and went across to greet them at the hotel door, when Ann almost put a half nelson on me and bundled me out. I retaliated and said, 'I can welcome Mhairi if I wish.' 'Well, take her across to the house,' she said. Bossy besom, I thought, to hang with the dinner, I'd rather have a cup of tea at home. I took Mhairi across and she had a bowl of soup. Conversation was nil, too much emotion between us no doubt, grief took over, I little knew there was extra worry as well. They came and went across for cups of coffee and then I suggested: 'Would it not be a good thing if they all disappeared and let George and I have time to wash and dress.' I reluctantly opened the wardrobe door and decided on a velvet two piece I had already worn at a WRI dinner, at least some of the family had not seen it, and no rural ladies to be there – or so I thought.

We were ordered to stay put till Grant, our grandson, was to come across for us, which he did, but said Sybil and family were to be a bit late on arriving and the dinner was to be put back till later. We sat back, glad of the respite.

They eventually arrived, all six of them plus Jason, and I thought a bomb had struck the place. Jeans were discarded, 'Granny where's your iron?' 'Where can I plug in the hot brush?' 'I'm starving.' Toilet and bathroom bombarded, thank goodness we were already dressed. George pacing up and down saying, 'Why can't we go across?' 'No way,' said I, 'and leave all this muddle and may be an iron left on or a hot brush on the carpet.' Eventually peace reigned in the house and Grant and Scott came across for us to escort us through the puddles in the road and we both made for the dining room. 'No, this way,' said the host. 'They are in the lounge.'

I mentioned earlier in my book, I never did like drinks before my meal and I literally stamped my way along that corridor, because by this time, I was hungry and possibly angry.

The scene that met our eyes dispelled our hunger and anger. In the next few seconds with the strains of 'Anniversary Waltz' coming from a band, I felt like the astronauts 'floating'. I certainly did not know where my feet were, as George and I were pushed together to waltz. We did not dance, we leant on one another. Why my enlarged heart did not burst I do not know. In the dimly lit room one face confronted me, I could not believe it was true, that she was there. Winnie, my eighty-five year old friend had been confined to bed all week and I took a walk over daily to see her. There she was sitting bright as a button and all I could say when I did reach her was, 'Are you wise, woman?'

I mentioned earlier that cameras do not usually lie and they certainly did not that night. The expression of awe and disbelief on my face was well registered, as I took in the scene around, especially the coloured faces of my relatives from London whom I had not seen since they were children. I was in so much shock, it took a week to register what happened, how it happened, the secrecy of it all, why Ann almost manhandled me out of the hotel door in the afternoon in case I spotted any of the guests. It would be good for somebody else to describe the events of the evening, because there was resentment running through me all the time: if I knew so and so, this is not what I would have worn, I did not like my short hair cut etc. My neighbour Margaret, said cheerio in the morning, 'We're away to Dundee for the weekend, see and have a nice time with the family!' And there she was laughing her head off at us.

It must have been the best kept secret in Rannoch as everybody knew about it but us, and arrangements had been made since September. Two young grandchildren must have been well rewarded for keeping quiet.

Why two Golden Wedding cakes? This so puzzled us as we went to cut the cake, the camera man certainly captured the wondering expression on my face! I later learnt that Ann had been making the cake when she urgently had to go up to Stirling when Colin was ill. A friend thought she would not be able to complete the task, so she made one.

Amongst the sea of faces I was looking for one and eventually had the courage to ask, 'Have you forgotten Mary, our bridesmaid?' No, through family illness she could not come; and there were others who I thought might have been there and possibly overlooked, but I realised that my family could not possibly have known all my friends, so should any of them ever read this, belated apologies.

I can recall as I eventually sat in a stupor, how much the young and old seemed to be enjoying themselves. I was peeved that I could no longer dance. It continued long after midnight and I said to my friends who came from the north west coast like myself, 'Do you realise what you are doing, dancing and drinking into the Sabbath morning?' 'Oh,' they said, 'they are long dead those that would disapprove!' 'Well,' I said, 'I am off home, you enjoy yourselves,' only to discover somebody had the key of our house and no way were we to get in. I demanded I needed it for my medication. 'It's all up in the Bridal Suite,' I was told, night clothes, pills etc. My nightie turned out to be the slip I discarded on the bed while I was dressing, and George's pyjama jacket only, no slippers, no dressing gown. George could not have cared less, he was full of whisky, I was sober but he could have lain down in clothes, shoes, the lot.

George went into the toilet attached to the bedroom, I heard the plug being pulled and I was desperate to get in. Waiting on him coming out, I opened the door to see if he was OK, and the sight that I beheld would have knocked me sober if I had been drunk. He was actually putting his hands in the toilet and then drying them on the towel. Oh, I thought, he really is drunk, he does not know the difference between the loo and the wash hand basin. I said to him, 'Are you alright?' 'Of course I am,' he slurred. 'Well, do you realise what you have just done?' 'What?' he said. 'You mistook the toilet for the wash hand basin,' 'I did not!' he said. 'I saw you put your hands in the loo,' I said. 'Well,' he said, 'I dropped

97

two one pound coins in there.' Seemingly he stood and took out his wallet to count what money he had left, in the wallet was loose change and he dropped two of the coins in the toilet. I was hysterical with laughter and knew there was no way I was going to sleep this night. Fortunately Ann came along and knocked on the door and shouted, 'Are you alright?' 'Certainly I am not!' I shouted, 'Come in and get me a large whisky or I will go crackers.' I told her the tale and asked who took across our supposed night attire. 'I don't know,' she said and then she went into hysterics. I had a good story to tell at breakfast time, much to George's annoyance.

All the jigsaw pieces were beginning to form a pattern. I was desperate to get across to our own house for proper footwear, but who had the key? Oh, Sybil – hadn't all her crew slept in West View, hence us decanted from our own bed. After breakfast I discovered all those lovely gifts we received produced from what must have been the strong room of the hotel, all those had to be taken across and opened carefully. Can you imagine the boorach (shambles) in West View! The discarded jeans etc, the wrappings of the gifts, where could I go for solace? The church I thought, yes and who do you think followed me, most of the guests, they had stayed in the hotel. I did not hear a word of the sermon, I was thinking, how do I feed this lot! Then I had a brain-wave. Get quickly back to the hotel and see if they can do sandwiches for thirty odd. Was I grateful for them to say yes! Everybody in more than good spirits till midnight again, at least I would be in my own bed tonight.

Monday morning was more than welcome as I felt like one of the balloons they'd decorated our house with, slowly getting smaller and smaller. As I have already said, it took a week for me to digest it all, and I am sure Ann would qualify for the Badge of the SAS for organising that celebration and keeping it a secret. I hope the family realized how much we appreciated it all a few weeks afterwards.

After the excitement of the Golden Wedding which left everybody on a high, I had cause for concern as I never did like too much of a high because in my life there always came a low. At the celebrations everybody was in exuberant mood, except Mhairi, and I naturally put it down to the fact that the only one missing in the family tree was darling Paula. I could have accepted that as the reason but unfortunately it was not the cause. Two days afterwards she had to disclose that it had been verified that she had breast cancer. This I thought was cruel, as she had been still battling with her grief.

The mother instinct in me rose strongly so I said, no matter what my commitments were to support her so I went to her home and after her operation accompanied her daily for her radium treatment. George was once more left to paddle his own canoe which he was more than willing to do and kept our home on an even keel for a month. In such cases the phone is a boon when George would enquire what he would have for dinner tomorrow or where were his grey socks. Our daily visits to the hospital educated me in another aspect of life as while I was waiting on Mhairi I met so many brave people, sad people and from all walks of life that made me count my blessings for my life.

With love and family support Mhairi soon got over this latest hurdle and in no time at all got engrossed in her work again and even took on a more responsible job as manageress of a shop.

Now I was looking forward to what could be described as a high. It was Colin's last year at university – would he make it? He had a few hiccups along the way, change of carers, broken shoulder etc, but he is tough and I knew he would overcome all these to qualify. When he did unfortunately I did not feel well enough at the time to go through to his graduation but all his aunts supported his parents that day and his photo in his graduation gown is superb. Sitting there with that wonderful smile nobody would know he was disabled. Now for the job hunting and as he said, 'Gran, the able bodied have a steep hill to climb, what do you think mine is to be like. I have the added burden of overcoming the entrance to buildings but all I can do is keep on trying.' His brothers left home to go to a Home for the Disabled and managed to get suitable employment to serve their needs. Colin had a much more active brain, inherited genes from the MacKenzie or Hughes? I dare not say. He was much more adventurous and as Wales did not seem to come up with the goods he set his sights on London. Earlier in my story you may recall I said everybody was heading for London much to my annoyance, being a real boiled in the bag SNP. It took nearly a year of letter writing, topping up his parents' phone bill before he arrived at what he wanted; a job with Radio 4. Where? – London of course. I did not care though, it could have been Barcelona as long as he got what he qualified for. You will note I speak about highs and lows so what was my low that year? Poor Mairi's trouble reared its ugly head again but she is not christened Mairi MacKenzie for nothing and again she fought that battle bravely and got back to work as soon as she could.

I mentioned earlier on no matter what age your family are you are always a mother and it hurts not to be able to bear the burdens your family have. If only you could take them all on board. It certainly would help if one was born with a silver spoon in one's mouth, which I was not, so I could not help them financially. The years began to take their toll of George and me and the long journey to Wales was hopeless, for both distance and finance. It should and could have been so much more rewarding if I could drop in, make Ann sit down and get on with the ironing, hang out the wash or keep Lyn company while Ann could go into town.

The next thing to occupy my mind was where was Lyn going to get a job. As Colin pointed out, access to buildings was a very important factor. Lyn applied to a local hospital as a contracting clerk, the advert carried the new Employment Service Symbol with the pledge that the Authority is an equal opportunity employer and is committed to employ people with disabilities. She had her first interview and was back for a second which went well. She was then taken to see the new disabled toilet in the scanner unit and it was totally unsuitable for a wheelchair bound person. She was turned down as she could not lift heavy medical records from shelves. Why was it left until after the interview stage of the medical until one of the most fundamental aspects of the job description from her point of view was brought to her attention? She felt her intelligence had been insulted and that she had been discriminated against on the grounds of her disability. The inaccessibility of toilets in a hospital of all places! If that was her experience in a local place for a job there was little hope of one elsewhere unless in good old London town. Like her brother, Colin, she will keep on trying. How galling for her to have the brains only to find circumstances and designs of buildings restrict her from using them. For all the advancement in this modern world there is not much in the architecture of buildings to cater for the disabled, not even in the dips in pavements for wheelchairs to enter buildings or shops.

What was the next thing to look forward to? Why should I expect any? But on recalling all the offspring I saw at the Golden Wedding something was bound to happen amongst the family. The advantage of a Golden Wedding is that the youngest of the grandchildren are there also and it is so interesting to see three generations and you are proud to be grandparents. Before we could fully appreciate all that, Graham made us great grandparents. Did we feel any older? – No. He brought his son over from Germany and we were thrilled to hold wee Glen, what blessings were bestowed us. Not to be outdone, David decided to marry and he produced a son – all these boys again.

Well, there is not much more to write about. I have spoken about the birth of my own children, our grandchildren and now our great grandchildren. Why did I start writing this book in the first instance? I always liked scribbling, writing letters being my hobby and then little articles for a northern paper. From this I made contact with many of my school pals whom I had not seen or written to since our school days. Later on I will mention how I am indebted to that same northern paper. I wrote a little article about life between two crofts as a child and my Muscular Dystrophy grandchildren read it and said, 'Surely you are not going to stop at that, Granny, after all the stories we have heard from you? Please do write some more.' I was persuaded by Colin and Lyn to do so and said if I ever get it published any monies would go to M.D. research. It has not been easy to do so, how do I get the inspiration and when? Mostly during the nights the present words are produced at 2 a.m. as I cannot sleep. I can usually store them but if it is convenient I rise, have a cup of tea and jot them down. It is many months since I wrote the last chapter as many unfortunate incidents have occurred but not worthwhile writing about – who wants to hear about arthritic joints?

I had always yearned to go back to the croft in the hills and the croft by the sea and also George's roots in the Black Isle. Public transport was by now out of the question for us but Shelagh, my fifth daughter, whom I almost threw in the Tay seeing she was not a boy, came up trumps. She must have guessed our thoughts and asked if we'd like to visit our birthplaces. Though a busy hairdresser, she shut her salon and we all set off to see the places and folks we talked about. One of the ports of call was my parents' gravestone which she cleared for us while George and I walked through the graveyard, saddened to see so many of my school pals, and friends, names on the stones. We wondered how many were left to visit in the village. Suffice to say enough for us to go into deep nostalgia and for Shelagh to witness and see and savour a way of life we'd spoken about. To the younger generation it is not that exciting to be in the company of elderly parents but she had to admit that she laughed more in four days than she had in the last four years, ending up with what I would describe as belly ache and shoulder ache. She saw a way of life in the Highlands she did not even understand: people's quotations, people's way of life, people's outlook on life and people's kindness. I was glad she had experienced that as she could not understand how such a strong bond could still exist between people you had not seen for over 50 years, and having been there when I met some old school pals she commented she could not visualise the same happening to her if she met up with somebody she had been at school with thirty years on. I said it must be the Highland blood. To me to get back to the croft in the hills was like winning the pools and to have my photo taken at the door again was such a thrill. It's funny that the simplest pleasures in life cost so little. Shelagh was fascinated that I got such a welcome from the then village G.P. of 50 odd years ago (now retired), and that he could remember me and still continue the argument or discussion we had when my first born Ann was delivered. On being called out when I was in labour (a home birth) he studied my progress for a while and then announced he would have to leave me and go to see an elderly Laird who was very ill with pneumonia – no antibiotics in those days – about three miles away. He said, 'You will be all right till I come back.' I felt anything but all right and thought how horrible that this newly qualified 25 year old should leave me at a time like this and said so – just to pander to the wealthy to whom he could charge more. No health service then. In hindsight I knew he was right not to stand there for the next few hours between my contractions, but he was thoughtful enough to contact the District Nurse who came for hours to support me. Why did we discuss such an incident after all his deliveries since then? Because I was one of his first deliveries and though an 80 year old with a failing memory he recalled I had left the district and was interested to know how many of a family I had. On hearing I had five daughters he said, 'By that time you did not need a doctor.'

The weather in the north-west was equal to Mediterranean temperatures which made the venture even more enjoyable and we were so grateful to Shelagh and were now content to make it our last journey there. I think she more or less agreed that we were certainly not fit for any more of these ventures without somebody's help.

Being a keen W.R.I. member I always entered competitions and wrote small articles to the magazine. I entered the Warnoch Trophy which is open to all members of the Scottish W.R.I.'s, based on 'A Day in the life of a member' in not more than 600 words. I again took an incident in a day in the life on the croft in my present area. I was quite surprised and at the same time delighted to win the trophy, more for the sake of our federation. Again this brought some letters from members throughout Scotland congratulating me. I had already had a pen pal from New Zealand a few years previously who read an article in a W.R.I. magazine that landed out there.

One dreich February a buff coloured envelope arrived addressed to Mary MacDonald, Journalist, Kinloch Rannoch. 'Oh,' I said, 'this sounds good.' On the back of the envelope was a Malta address. I thought the W.R.I. magazine even gets out there, another contact – maybe even a holiday in Malta! I opened it casually and after ten minutes I was rooted to the spot with the information it contained. I understood that I had met all my nieces and nephews in this world and here was the prospect of meeting one I never knew existed. I stared at the birth certificate, death certificate etc and realised that my sister, Ann, who died in London in 1938 had given birth to a son three months before that. None of us had ever known. He had a lonely bewildered life from his adopted parents and was never told the truth as to who he was. He travelled the world with the Navy and latterly with an oil company but had the courtesy to come home to London at the time of his adopted mother's death. In her effects he found some very interesting information such as a letter written by his blood Granny, my mother, thanking the landlady for letting her know that Ann was in hospital. His base being in Malta, the Wester Ross address was like a dot in the ocean to him. He set off in mid winter to investigate but his grandparents being dead for over 40 years it was not easy for the locals to give him any information as there were not many of that era alive. Luckily he did come across one local who knew of Ian's grandfather and took him to the graveyard to see the family headstones including his own natural mother's as her remains were brought home. On asking this man if he knew of any living relatives he was told there was one in Kinloch Rannoch but did not know her address. However, on looking at a map he gathered Kinloch Rannoch was a small place and having been told she wrote articles for the northern paper he thought if he addressed it as Mary MacDonald, Journalist, it would arrive. Weather conditions on both road and rail did not allow him time to detour to me as he had to catch a plane from Edinburgh. It took him several weeks to gather information such as birth certificate, dates, a copy of my mother's letter, the writing which brought me to tears and then into shock for several hours.

I did mention in an earlier chapter that I began to sense that there was something I had not yet achieved, that something was missing, that I may have been ready to leave this world before realising what it was. Was this it? I being the only one left of the family to give the needed information to Ian that he did belong to a family and a very loving one and bring much needed happiness to somebody searching for their roots, my mother's letter being the only link kept in a box for 50 years. I calmed myself down, got an airmail letter and wrote as much information as I could and told him that he really was one of us. I did not have any information about him and waited several weeks for a reply. Then one evening in May I had a phone call from Malta to say he had got my letters on his return from the Philippines where he'd been in his capacity as a trouble shooter with an oil company. He was thrilled to hear my voice and promised to come to Scotland as soon as he could. This would take almost a year. I was getting impatient as I had a few hiccups with my health and was desperate to see if I could see a family resemblance. However, I did live to see him and Judy and what an emotional meeting it was. It is so good to see a man of over 50 years with tears of joy in his eyes and at the same time, sad at how much he has missed out on but thrilled and overcome to find so many relations. He was annoyed at the waste of time the many times he was berthed in Scotland, Rosyth, Montrose and Glasgow and did not know his kith and kin so near. There was so much I wanted to know that normally curiosity required me to ask twenty questions but this required a hundred and twenty. I am sure by this time he must have felt he should have stayed in isolation. On first setting eyes on him I was overjoyed especially knowing he was the son of loveable, good looking Ann who unfortunately had seemingly blotted her copy book in London and did not have the courage to tell her parents or brothers and sisters. Bringing an illegitimate child into the thirties was very very much frowned upon and no doubt when TB was discovered at the time of birth this was an added noose around her neck. She died three months later. My heart is sore when I dwell on the circumstances. To think that George and I with five daughters could have had an adopted son. He seemingly was registered as Ian MacKenzie but his name was changed. However, I am so grateful that I lived to give Ian all the information he required and he is equally grateful. He wants us out to the sunshine of Malta but we have, I think, crossed a bridge too far and content if spared to have another visit from him.

I have been running out of material for this book but that unexpected news, though a shock, gave me more material and once again I mentioned that I was indebted to the monthly paper of the north for him to have been able to trace me. Ian felt bitter about the lack of information from his adopted family but I tried to point out to him that maybe his mother swore them to secrecy and they had seemingly lost their own second son and he was a replacement. He maintains they could have given him information after the time of his grandparent's death. Maybe so but his adopted parents are gone and he cannot question them now.

Sadness and gladness filters through my life. My grandson, Edward, is now married and we managed to go to that enjoyable day but his mother, Mhairi, still keeps fighting that dreaded disease. So my highs and lows come like a see-saw but glad I am of each day that I still manage to care for George whom the birthdays are taking a toll of. He still gets his bright days like winning a Hi-Fi in a raffle, local football wins and finding his ring lost in the garden three years ago. He says, 'Well, I am meant to live to enjoy these things.'

I do not feel there is any more to write about but to thank our blessings for all our offspring because the material things we have acquired by pressing buttons do not mean much. My faith and spiritual guidance is what is now important and my main and dearest wish is for the world to find a cure for muscular dystrophy and cancer which has dimmed my horizon for years.

Epilogue

I finished that chapter and felt I had little more to write about, or rather – plenty to write about but no time to do so. My mind and body were overloaded, my time drawn both ways to the two I loved, I realised that time was short. The dreaded disease reappeared in Mhairi despite the fact she went through the terrible ordeal of chemotherapy and had a glimmer of hope. George by this time was now weakening, his poor old lungs refusing to take any more. I did not have to decide whom I should support as fate took over and I took fluid on the knee which reduced me to crutches for several weeks. Those weakening tried to give me courage as I was suffering a lot of pain but they were not – I do not want to remember '92.

As the weeks went by I wondered which of my loved ones I was to lose first. I am sure George would have been willing to say goodbye if it left us with Mhairi a bit longer but things do not work that way. She tried hard to hold on till Christmas but she was buried on the 23rd December. Though a frail man and ill, George was determined to be at her graveside and he was, against doctor's orders, and that virtually was the end of him. He was heartbroken and his spirit was gone. He still held on till Easter Saturday but had to be hospitalised for the last two weeks of his life. However we had the pleasure of all the family with him day and night for five days which he really loved and we were all thankful to kiss him goodbye aged 83 years. Much credit and gratefulness we award to P.R.I. for the generous hospitality they gave us all week and the loving care and attention they all gave George which helped us in our grief.

What do I do now? Bound more or less to somebody for 55 years what do I occupy my time with? At this point I do not know as there is a restriction on what I can do, certain conditions do not allow me to do things I would like to. George's passing does not bow me down with grief as we had such a long rewarding life busy life. Mhairi's passing has saddened me a lot but at the same time my life seems very empty and if only I was stronger I would love to help others in need. I can only do this verbally or by expression. I do love company and people and hope that those who do visit me feel better and happier as they come away. Kindness can be shown in one's eyes or in one's warm greeting and many are going to miss George for his warm welcome. They quote 'this house will not be the same without George' – no insult to me. I am glad to hear them say it as I know it is said with sincerity.

I pondered as to how to keep his memory alive for others. Not for long. His passing coincided with the warm weather coming when he used to sit in the village square, but no George this year. With permission from the Region we installed a wrought iron seat in his memory and baskets of flowers attached. His ashes were scattered up Loch Rannoch side. These two lovely spots are imprinted on my mind at present. How many people I have tried to console in their grief but now I know it was only words and I could not possibly visualise their feelings. I do now but as Shakespeare quoted: 'Give sorrow words; the grief that does not speak, Whispers the o'er fraught heart and bids it break.'

You may think all my burdens are now past – not so. My mind throughout these anxious weeks with Mhairi and George's illnesses carried the knowledge that Lyn, my granddaughter with muscular dystrophy, 400 miles away, was having a very traumatic time following trying to overcome a virus which rendered her pretty helpless. She had to be hospitalised for weeks. Think of the anguish of her mother who could not leave her to visit her dying sister. Happily Lyn recovered enough to let her mother come to her father's bedside and give him much joy in his last days, so there was not any clear definition of anything on my mind, just a fuzz. That has now partly cleared and my immediate thoughts are with Lyn and her parents. She is now reduced to being dependent on a ventilator so no matter what cheery thoughts or deeds become part of my life, there is always that cloud which appears in my mind when thinking of Lyn and I wish that I was near her. People are always asking me to go and visit them and have a holiday but for the present my own little cosy nest is my castle. I do not like to leave it meantime and then return to an empty house. During the winter of my worries and exhaustion of nursing George somebody asked me if I believed in God. Of course I do, I said, it is He who is helping me through this bad spell. For trials such as this knock us off our proud pedestals and lead us to rely on God. Sometimes God uses suffering to help us to relate to others who are suffering.

George's words of wisdom I used to scoff at but now the reality of them is brought home to me in many ways. In what I could call my freedom I do not do anything he would be displeased about and try to keep the arrangements we both had. Unfortunately he did not live to enjoy the promise of sunshine in Malta. Is that going to be my next venture, I wonder? There are a few things I would like to do mindwise but the body says no. One is I must try and finish this book for the sake of my grandchildren whom I have been blessed to see, so that I can give them a very special sense of who they are and where they come from. As one grandson said to me: It's a gift no one else could have given me and I will always treasure it. I am like a clocking hen, I would like to be within touching distance of them all, not that they would maybe want that.

It's so interesting to note likenesses and habits in the generations that follow. I am a person who likes all people and is interested in people's mannerisms and attitudes more so than in their looks. Conversation is a stimulant to me. Knowing this part of me the family has once more steered me towards the WRI which I more or less had to forget about over the last year with attending to George. I had always been a member and was quite willing to attend again after I had a period of much needed rest. I thought that after being a member for nearly 58 years I was quite willing to sit back and enjoy it. It did not turn out that way. Like many other organisations that were going into liquidation. This one was threatening to do so. With much arm twisting and offers of help I am back as President meantime and gey rusty with it, I don't have the same fervour as before. We have a lot of competition now with Educational Classes which is good for those requiring a change. The Scottish Women's Rural Institution is the only organisation in Scotland with educational and charitable status. SWRI is a non party political, non sectarian movement which is linked internationally with many country women's societies in countries all the world over by the organization known as The Associated Country Women of the World of which the SWRI is a constituent member. It is not a gossipy women's evening out as most men think of it.

I know children tend to think of parents as rather asexual, especially teenage grandchildren would think in that light. I produced a love letter from their grandfather to me written in his sixties, a time when he had to be away from home and missing me a lot. I saw that little sly grimace on their faces, maybe a little jealousy, to learn that there was another kind of love other than the one he poured on them. They possibly thought what on earth has she held on to them for? Why did I? Was it that I always thought one day they might be a comfort to me and so they are. I always remember my mother holding on to a letter that my late sister Anne wrote and in Gaelic quoted, 'To think that piece of paper outlasts the human being'. I have always held on to letters – my mother's last letter, my brother Colin's last letter, not knowing it was to be their last; Mhairi's last birthday card to me; it is so comforting to see their writing. Fantasies and fallacies can be equally strong but they do not last.

Recalling wartime, I mentioned we used to have Italian prisoners of war to work on the farm, and with the meagre amenities of wartime it was all hard work and no pleasure rearing three children and helping my husband outside as well, no social life whatsoever so when one Italian prisoner, Cammerite Giovanni, 25 years of age, took a shine to me it was time to take a second look in the mirror. I was also 25 years of age and I then began to live in a world of fantasy and thought, 'If only this and if only that, if only I was not married with three kids'. But it never got any further than sitting together in the back of the bogey going tattie picking and a squeeze of the hand. Good job repatriation came soon! You will recall I cried when the train taking them away home passed our cottage and the blankets left at the door with the note – thanks and love. I have a letter received after he got home with the main ingredient being the thanks for all things he would always love, always remember, never forget, letter dated 19 June 1945. He certainly forgot as that was the only letter which was written to us both as it began, Dear Friends. No doubt as soon as he got home he came down from cloud nine. I taught them a lot of English words with the help of my oldest child's books. To me I was mothering those boys, trying to produce spaghetti and macaroni for them but to Cammerro I was no mother. They were allowed one evening away from the camp so used to come along for supper. I would like to meet them all in old age. I must have handled that letter many times as it is gey flimsy now so it is good he did not stay in the country or I might have been writing about my latin lover instead of what I have written because no man other than George made me look in the mirror twice.

I keep writing about my daily life and not much mention of the outside world. It is so topsy turvey one cannot keep up with it and I am glad I am the age I am as it is all so frightening. Neil Kinnock, George's hero, was knocked off his pedestal before George's passing so he was not interested any more in politics. Now his pal, Andy Stewart the singer, has passed away this week. That would also have been a downer for him. I kept looking at the photo of him and Andy taken here about five years ago by Andy's teenage daughter and feel sad that Andy should really leave us the same year as George, and him only 59 years of age. What does it all mean, badly divided, as the tinks used to say. My theory is that life is a raffle with so many tickets pulled every day so we should make the most of every day we are given and not waste it. I am now stuck for material and I only hope I can get this book published to give any monies to M.D. research but will leave it open in case something interesting or unexpected happens: life is full of surprises, anything could happen.

Now I have received the best news that '93 could have given me so far, not the winning of the pools, but the knowledge that my memoirs are accepted for publishing. I had always hoped but so many also have had the same idea, and not being a celebrity I knew my chances were slim and I would possibly just have left them behind like a diary for my offspring.

I must pay tribute to my grandchildren Colin Hughes and Lyn Hughes M.D. who coaxed me along and helped with the typing etc. and also the encouragement of the rest of the families who often at the same time criticised my shorthand vocabulary, often finishing my sentences with 'Bla Bla Bla', much to their annoyance.

I would also like to put in print the support of the local Doctor and his assistant which they gave me over the last year when nursing George was almost beyond me.

There is a funny side to everything, George's last hours at home were very emotional, he did not want to go to hospital, naturally he was crying, saying 'Why are you putting me away? I have loved you all my life?'

I said, 'If the Doctor had the necessary equipment here he would not need to.'

'Well,' he replied, 'it's time he had.' But it was too late for anything. I went to get his suitcase packed before the ambulance arrived, and on my return to the bedroom I witnessed something I never thought I would. The Doctor lying down beside George almost into a caress and coaxing him. 'Well!' I said, 'I have seen it all now, two men in a bed together in my house! Get up!' That broke the emotional scene. I appreciated the gesture of the doctor, who was very fond of George, only a village doctor would have done that. Bless him.

If George is in the Spirit World he will be sprouting wings. He always said, 'You are so good with the pen, Mary.' My last parting shot is I am so proud of Colin who is well established at Radio 4 in London. I saw him on television last week. Grandpa's quote would have been, 'You are hardy Colin.'